REACH TO RECOVERY

REACH TO RECOVERY: DEPRESSION ANONYMOUS

BY MARILYN PATTERSON

AUSTIN, TEXAS

REACH TO RECOVERY: DEPRESSION ANONYMOUS
BY MARILYN PATTERSON

Cover Artwork © Jonathan Qualben
www.jonathanqualben.com (see page 139)
Cover Graphics: Michael Qualben

PUBLISHED BY
LANGMARC PUBLISHING
P.O. 90488
AUSTIN, TEXAS 78709-0488
1-800-864-1648

Library of Congress Control Number: 2004106434
ISBN: 1-880292-688   U.S.A. $13.95; Canada: $17.95

CONTENTS

PART ONE: THE PROGRAM

PART II: PERSONAL STORIES

APPENDIXES

INTRODUCTION

I hope every person suffering from depression and bipolar disorder will read this book and find relief and hope. This book is also intended as a manual for those interested in starting a Depression Anonymous group. There is a great need for support groups like Depression Anonymous; an article in the February 21, 2003 edition of *The Houston Chronicle* underscores this need:

> The World Health Organization has identified depression as the disease with the fourth heaviest burden to society and predicts that it will become the second leading cause of disability worldwide by 2020 . . . unless strides are made in prevention, diagnosis and treatment.[1]

Clearly we need to be doing more to stop the epidemic of depression and to help those who suffer from it.

Over the past ten years, I have attended probably over 800 meetings of Alcoholics Anonymous. (I have two close family members that are members of A.A., and I am a member of Al-Anon.) The power of Twelve-Step programs to change people's lives has astounded me. When I began attending A.A. to support my family members, I applied all the principles of A.A. to the special problems I face as a depression-prone person.

I began to notice an increased feeling of well-being, lengthened periods of happiness, longer and longer intervals between the times I needed to be on antidepressant medication. I attribute this vast improvement to the power of working the Twelve Steps.

I observed people around me who admitted they were suffering from depression. Most were on antidepressant medication and had a very passive attitude, as though they were saying, "My depression is my doctor's problem; it's up to him to prescribe the right medication. The disease is too baffling for me; my entire trust is in the right pill."

I used to have this attitude until an experience in 1989 caused an important shift. I was in a therapy group at that time and complaining to them that my depression had returned. I was feeling very angry and sorry for myself and was expecting to get barrels of sympathy.

Carol spoke right up. "I don't feel sorry for you. You bring these depressions on yourself."

Deluged with anger, I thought, "How could she be so insensitive and uncaring?"

As I was driving home, however, the thought hit me, "What if she is right? What if I am doing something to bring on these spells of depression? What if I could change some things and no longer get so depressed?"

The upshot was that I went to the library and checked out thirteen books on depression. If there were something I could do or something I could change that would impact the disease, I wanted to know about it.

This marked the beginning of my active part in recovery. I discovered that there were indeed some changes I could make. I started eating more nutritious meals and taking vitamins. I began walking more. I organized a small *ad hoc* mental health support group. I resolved to do everything in my power to get better.

This attitude is essential for recovery from depression. If depressed people would apply the same energy and dedication to relieving their depression that I have observed in members of A.A., their lives would be more fulfilled and happier.

Other important considerations: An estimated 20 percent of people are not helped at all by antidepressant medication. Some cannot take antidepressants because of other medical conditions, and there are those who are on antidepressant medication who still feel depressed. What can be done for these people to bring hope and joy back to their lives?

This book was written for these people. If you are one of these, go through each step in the book and write out your own answers to the "QUESTIONS TO ASK MYSELF" section as well as any thoughts that might cross your mind as you are studying each step. This will be your own personal journal of recovery.

In addition, I urge you to form a Depression Anonymous group. All you need is a meeting place and two or three like-minded people to begin. Most churches will donate space; newspapers and mental health centers will inform the public. There is a power in Twelve-Step group meetings that no one has been able to measure scientifically but is nevertheless dynamic and life changing.

---

[1] Associated Press, *Houston Chronicle*, "Long-Term Antidepressants Cut Relapse Risk, Study Finds," February 21, 2003, p. 12A.

BASIC FACTS ABOUT THE PROGRAM

Depression Anonymous is a fellowship of people who have experienced in the past or are currently experiencing depression. We believe in sharing our experience, strength and hope regarding this illness. We believe that changed attitudes can aid recovery.

Depression Anonymous is not allied with any sect, denomination, political entity, organization, or institution, does not engage in any controversy, neither endorses nor opposes any causes. There are no dues for membership. Depression Anonymous is self-supporting through voluntary contributions.

Depression Anonymous has but one purpose: to alleviate the suffering of people afflicted with depression. We do this by practicing the Twelve Steps and by giving understanding and encouragement to those around us. We believe that we can depend on a "Power greater than ourselves" for help in solving our problems and finding relief from depression.

Thus depending on God, Depression Anonymous has certain assumptions:

1. That God desires us to experience fullness of joy and gladness; God does not desire us to be immobilized with sadness and depression.

2. That God desires us to love ourselves and our neighbors. When we fail to do this, any feeling of sadness is meant as a "wake-up call" for us to change our attitudes or our behavior. This is the sadness of legitimate guilt, and it is intended to spur us to make amends (see steps four through eight). The free-floating sadness of depression that hovers over us, unrelated to any positive corrective action, is not of God.

This program operates on the supposition that we sometimes sink into periods of depression when we stray in our thoughts and behavior from the path that

God intends. We forget to be grateful for all the blessings God has bestowed on us. We look with envy at other people. We harbor resentments against God, life, people and things. We ignore our conscience, do wrong, and try to rationalize our bad feelings away. We don't take the proper responsibility for our behavior. We forget that we always have a choice in any situation—even in our thoughts.

THE TWELVE STEPS OF
ALCOHOLICS ANONYMOUS

1. We admitted we were powerless over alcohol—that our lives had become unmanageable.
2. Came to believe the at Power greater than ourselves could restore us to sanity.
3. Made a decision to turn our will and our lives over to the care of God *as we understood Him*.
4. Made a searching and fearless moral inventory of ourselves.
5. Admitted to God, to ourselves, and to another human being the exact nature of our wrongs.
6. Were entirely ready to have God remove all these defects of character.
7. Humbly asked Him to remove our shortcomings.
8. Made a list of all persons we had harmed, and became willing to make amends to them all.
9. Made direct amends to such people wherever possible, except when to do so would injure them or others.
10. Continued to take personal inventory and when we were wrong promptly admitted it.
11. Sought through prayer and meditation to improve our conscious contact with God *as we understood Him*, praying only for knowledge of His will for us and the power to carry that out.
12. Having had a spiritual awakening as the result of these steps, we tried to carry this message to alcoholics and to practice these principles in all our affairs.

The Twelve Steps are reprinted and adapted with permission of Alcoholics Anonymous World Services, Inc. (A.A.W.S.) Permission to reprint and adapt the Twelve Steps does not mean that A.A.W.S. has reviewed or approved the contents of this publication, or that A.A.W.S. necessarily agrees with the views expressed herein. A.A. is a program of recovery from alcoholism only—use of the Twelve Steps in connection with programs and activities which are patterned after A.A., but which address other problems, or in any other non-A.A. context, does not imply otherwise.

TWELVE STEPS OF
DEPRESSION ANONYMOUS

1. We admitted that in the grip of depression we were powerless to change the feeling; our lives had become unmanageable.

2. Came to believe that a Power greater than ourselves could restore us to sanity.

3. Made a decision to turn our will and our lives over to the care of God, *as we understood Him.*

4. Made a searching and fearless moral inventory of ourselves.

5. Admitted to God, to ourselves and to another human being the exact nature of our wrongs.

6. Were entirely ready to have God remove all these defects of character.

7. Humbly asked Him to remove our shortcomings.

8. Made a list of all persons we had harmed, and became willing to make amends to them all.

9. Made direct amends to such people whenever possible, except when to do so would injure them or others.

10. Continued to take personal inventory and when we were wrong promptly admitted it.

11. Sought through prayer and meditation to improve our conscious contact with God, *as we understood Him,* praying only for knowledge of His will for us and the power to carry that out.

12. Having had a spiritual awakening as the result of these steps, we tried to carry this message to others, and to practice these principles in all our affairs.

— PART ONE —

TWELVE STEPS OF DEPRESSION ANONYMOUS

STEP ONE

> "We admitted that in the grip of depression we were powerless to change the feeling; our lives had become unmanageable."

Many people can identify with the feeling of futility experienced when they try to get themselves out of a full-blown depression. "Snap out of it," people say to the depressed person, not realizing that the depressed person desperately wants to stop feeling the way he does. He starts to do things he formerly enjoyed only to feel blank and empty.

All of us who are depression-prone have at some time tried to feel better. Our methods vary—some drink alcohol, eat excessively, work longer hours, or have an affair in order to experience a "high." Many of our modern addictions have depression as a primary driving force.

Others try healthier ways to dispel the feeling of depression. Some people increase their social activities, take up a hobby, or develop a new interest. In the case of a mild depression, such activities may be successful. If the depression is severe (clinical), however, it seems as though the harder a person tries to rid himself of the depression, the more persistent the feeling becomes. The sufferer then finds himself in the position of being depressed because he is depressed.

Also implied in Step One is the acknowledgment that we are prone to depression; specifically we are "depressives"—people "affected with or prone to psychological depression."[1] Many fear that *admitting* they are depressives, the admission of weakness, is equivalent to *being* weak. The irony is that the admission of weakness is the first step to gaining real power. The powerlessness of the First Step lays the foundation for the true power to be found in Steps Two and Three.

The powerlessness addressed here is also a realization that we need help in recovering from depression — the measures we have taken previously to alleviate our depression have proved inadequate or downright futile.[2]

The second part of the first step is "that our lives had become unmanageable." The person in the grip of a depression experiences the leaden lethargy that makes even the simplest task seem monumental. Activities that he formerly performed easily and effortlessly now seem almost impossible. Sometimes he feels that he just can't get himself dressed and ready to work. He only feels like slumping over the TV set in his bathrobe for four or five days.

The managing part of the personality feels paralyzed, frozen in a strait jacket. Sometimes by a heroic act of willpower, the person can drive himself to do something absolutely essential—feed the baby, send in a report, get a few groceries, or pay the light bill. But the simplest effort is exhausting. The person is genuinely dismayed. Two weeks ago, he did all these things easily and naturally and didn't think anything about it. Now, everything seems like such a big effort. Unmanageability!

The first step is really an extension of the opening part of the Serenity Prayer—"God, grant me the serenity to accept the things I cannot change." Psychologists tell us that in truth we cannot really *change* any feeling by an act of will. With mild feelings of depression, we can distract ourselves from the feeling by certain activities, but this is not the same as changing the feeling.

When the depressed feeling becomes really strong and painful (clinical depression), it is essential that the depressed person consult his health-care professional. Usually, he will be given an antidepressant prescription. In most cases, the antidepressant medication does change the terrible feelings and allow the depressive to function again. Once recovery is on its way (and depression is a very treatable illness with about an 80 percent success rate), the principles of this program are useful to delay or prevent relapses.

This program focuses on the time before and after an intense depression when the person is feeling well enough to be teachable. It is the basis of this program that different ways of thinking and behaving will produce healthier results in the life of the depression-prone individual. Some people in this program have found their mood so much improved that anti-depression medication can be reduced. (This is an individual decision that should be guided by the person's health care professional.)

What is meant by a "teachable period" can best be explained by an analogy. Imagine that you somehow get a one-inch cut on your ankle. Being a health-conscious person, you would first cleanse the wound with antibacterial soap, hydrogen peroxide or alcohol. Then, you would probably put a bandage around the wound so that the dirt from the street would not drift up and cause an infection. You do all these healthy things, and the wound slowly heals. Soon, there is a slight scar, but you are as good as new.

In contrast, say that with the same cut, you make no effort to cleanse the wound. You walk around all day with the dirt and grime of the street blowing into the open wound. Soon, you have an infection, but still you do nothing. You go limping around on the sore leg. The infection gets worse, and eventually it's a life-threatening situation. If you're lucky, you are sent to a hospital and given strong antibiotics to counteract the infection. Hopefully, you do recover, but you could have avoided the whole hospital experience if you had just taken care of the wound in the beginning.

What the program of Depression Anonymous tries to do is to cleanse these emotional and spiritual wounds when they are fresh, so that the healing process can begin immediately, and the infection of depression is averted.

MEMBERS SHARE THEIR
EXPERIENCES WITH THIS STEP

I remember that it took a long time for me to realize that in the grip of depression I was powerless to change the feeling. I kept "dancing furiously around," trying this and that to banish the feeling. I prayed, I read the Bible, I went to social activities, I ate more, and I commiserated with friends who were also afflicted with depression. It seemed that the harder I ran from the feeling, the more relentlessly it pursued me.

Since mine was judged to be a clinical depression, my doctor prescribed Lithium and Tofranil. In a short time, I was feeling like my old self again. I experienced pleasure anticipating upcoming events. Getting up in the morning and beginning my day became almost effortless. My life was manageable once more.

While I was feeling better, I began practicing the principles of this program to prevent a relapse. I began writing a gratitude list to God of ten items each day. I did a fourth step inventory, writing down lurking resentments and other character flaws that I knew would contribute to a full-blown depression if I didn't deal with them.

In addition, Step One prompted me to accept without bitterness the fact that I have a physical predisposition to the disease of depression. Sometimes, on the slightest provocation, my brain chemicals become unbalanced, and I wake up with feelings of intense sadness, despair, futility, and at times thoughts of suicide. The disease produces these negative feelings.

The negative feelings are not reality; they are not the *real* me.

I am powerless to stop my body from reacting this way if I continually bombard my mind with resentful, fearful, ungrateful, and pessimistic thoughts. I am powerless to change this physical propensity, but I can accept this weakness, and (with the help of God) make some changes so that the disease does not take over my life.

QUESTIONS TO ASK MYSELF ABOUT
THE FIRST STEP

- Do I accept that in the grip of depression I am powerless to change the feeling?
- Am I willing to surrender the illusion that I can somehow change the intense feeling of depression?
- In the throes of depression, is my life unmanageable?
- What part of this chapter do I really identify with?
- What measures have I taken to alleviate my depression?
- Are these measures positive activities that can be productive or addictions to be avoided?

---

[1] *Merriam-Webster's Collegiate Dictionary* (Springfield, Massachusetts: Merriam-Webster, Inc., 2002).

[2] The word "powerless" is confusing to many people because one of the basic tenets of the Depression Anonymous program is that with the help of God we are empowered to change some of our thought and behavior patterns—and thereby to lessen depression. The important phrase is "with the help of God" (which is addressed in the Second and Third Steps).

— NOTES —

Step Two

> "Came to believe that a Power greater than ourselves could restore us to sanity."

"Came to believe" begins the step of hope. If all we had was Step One, we would be trapped in despair. Suicides are caught up with Step One because they stop there. The old proverb about the darkest hour being right before the dawn is helpful to remember at this point.

For those of us who came to the program with a belief in God, Step Two may seem a natural progression. What may be confusing to us is why God has allowed us to experience the disease of depression in the first place. This is one of those "why" questions that even the most brilliant theologians and philosophers have only an inadequate answer. Theologians call it "the problem of pain." If God is good, why do people (even seemingly *good* people) suffer?

Thousands of books have been written on this subject, and many find comfort in some of these books. When all is said and done, however, no one really knows the mind of God. This program takes the point of view that these "why" questions are best tabled. The fact is that people do experience the disease of depression—like they experience any number of diseases, like cancer, alcoholism, heart disease, diabetes, etc. The wise thing to do is to just accept that you have the disease, and that the power of God can assist you in dealing with it and restoring you to a healthier frame of mind.

In this program, we begin to learn how some of our own attitudes have impacted this disease. God reveals to us how some of our customary ways of thinking and behaving have set us up for a bout of depression.

This program makes no effort to define God—-the Power greater than ourselves. We have no specified theology. Most members say, however, that they have come to rely on a God of unconditional love—a kind, compassionate presence in their lives. This is not to say that any old behavior is permissible. Members find that the "God of their understanding" guides them in matters of decency and morality.

The difference that many members discover is that their God now is infinitely more patient, helpful and compassionate. Some members in the past had conceived of God as a perpetually angry, condemning judge—-ready to pounce on each tiny infraction. This progression to conceiving God as loving and helping has the net effect of making the member willing and eager to bring God into his everyday existence.

The second half of Step Two "could restore us to sanity" is a source of confusion to some members. "I've never been psychotic," one member told me the other day. "I've always been in touch with reality even though I was severely depressed."

In other twelve-step programs, we see a more dramatic form of insanity. The practicing alcoholic, dead drunk, does many strange things he would not do if he were sober. We're not talking about legal insanity, locked-ward mental hospital insanity. Nonetheless, some of us have experienced a major depression in the midst of what many would consider an ideal life—-isn't this a kind of insanity?

Members tell of feeling hopeless in life even though their actual situation looks promising to an outside observer. Members tell of feeling no pleasure in hobbies or activities that had formerly been great fun. They speak of a flatness, an inability to experience any pleasure in life. This may not qualify as legal insanity, but it is a deplorable situation from which members want to escape.

The sanity that the depression-prone person wants restored in his life is the sanity of a hopeful, meaningful, pleasurable existence. This is not too much to ask; this is precisely what the program is all about.

There is another dimension to sanity that the depression-prone person needs to consider. Sanity always implies that a person is in touch with reality. The depressive is usually in contact with outer reality but frequently is not really aware of his own inner reality.

Many depressives learn early in life to disassociate their real feelings from conscious awareness. They lie to themselves about what they are really feeling. After a while, they do not even realize that they are lying. This is where the rigorous honesty of the program clicks in. The depressive must be able to "own" his real feelings even though he doesn't like them.

MEMBERS SHARE THEIR
EXPERIENCES WITH THIS STEP

I spent a great deal of my life full of resentment against God because I found myself repeatedly confronted with the disease of depression. I felt that I had led a good life; I went to church; I prayed; I was active in the church. Why was it then that, about every three to six months for seemingly no reason, I was plunged into a pit of despondency and despair? In this pit I had no energy for the projects I had initiated when I was feeling good. Everything I did seemed a giant effort. Just getting out of bed and getting dressed was a major accomplishment. All I wanted to do was sit in front of the TV and stare at it for hours at a time.

However, I had many responsibilities at that time. I was expected to cook and clean for a husband and two children. I was enrolled in classes at a nearby college, so I needed to study each day. In my heart, I blamed my entire illness on God. I was consumed with resentment for God, for my husband, for my children, for life.

I remember once searching my soul for ONE positive feeling—*one* genuine thought of love—*one* admirable feeling I could latch onto so that I would not feel like such a worthless, evil wretch. I could not find a single worthy, benevolent feeling inside me.

Keep in mind that I was not acting on any of these angry feelings. I was still able to feed something to my husband and children; I managed to straighten the house enough so that life was not interrupted. But I had no positive feelings about any of it. When I was blatantly honest with myself, all my feelings were negative.

Some years later, I was able to see that it was the seething resentments inside me that fueled the depressions. God was not going to wave a magic wand over me and suddenly make my depressions disappear as long as I *chose* to hold on to my resentments and negative thoughts. When I could see the connection between these thoughts and my depression, I began to choose a healthier mental attitude.

Today, I strive to be very aware of resentments building up in my life because resentment-hoarding is perhaps my major flaw. Resentments for me are like the first drink for an alcoholic. I really cannot tolerate any. When angry feelings surface in my life, they must be dealt with immediately (see Fourth Step). The most important resentment I have banished is the one against God. Now I have truly come to believe that a Power greater than myself (whom I call God) is restoring me to sanity.

The sanity I now experience makes me examine my irate, bitter feelings in a new light. The last part of the Serenity Prayer, "the courage to change the things I can," is helpful advice at this point. For example, if I find myself resentful because of something that my husband is doing, I need to take some action. If I notice that he is speaking to me in a grumpy, irritated tone of voice, I might say to him: "Honey, all this week you've spoken to me in a grumpy, angry tone. What's wrong?"

Or, perhaps I know that my husband's best friend has just moved to a distant city, and he is still processing the loss of his friend. I might give him another week to snap out of it. But what I don't do anymore is totally ignore my angry feelings and pack them away in a mental "gunnysack." I either confront him about the situation, or I decide to accept the situation for now, *without resentment.*

As a result, I usually experience the sanity of a life filled with pleasure, hope, excitement, and joy.

QUESTIONS TO ASK MYSELF ABOUT
STEP TWO

- Do I find it difficult to believe in a Power greater than myself?
- Do I want a higher level of sanity in my life?
- How would I describe the God of my understanding?
- What part of this chapter do I need to process by writing in my journal?

— Notes —

STEP THREE

> **"Made a decision to turn our will and our lives over to the care of God as we understood Him."**

This is the central core of the entire program. In Steps One and Two we had come to the realization that our life under self-rule was intolerable. The rule of self had led us to this point of powerlessness, emptiness, and near despair. With something akin to desperation, we make the third-step decision.

The situation is similar to that of Audrey, a friend of mine. She had placed bird netting over a small tree in her front yard, and a robin became entangled in the netting. She tried to open the net so that the bird could fly away, but the robin didn't understand. Filled with fear, it went the wrong way and became hopelessly entangled. When the robin could no longer move, Audrey was able to free it so that it could fly away.

In this step, God frees us so that we are able to live happily again. It is helpful to contrast our lives lived under the domination of our depression-prone will and our lives lived under the care of God.

The depression-prone will is inclined primarily toward self-pity and self-centeredness. Behind self-pity is resentment against God. There is always the feeling that God hasn't provided the self with the money, good looks, friends, and special advantages that the self observes in others he perceives as better off. He feels *entitled* to all the "good things" he sees his neighbors enjoying; this self-pity is a prime breeding ground for depression.

Self-pity puts the depressive in the victim stance. The victim sees himself as essentially powerless before the vicissitudes of life. *And he is intensely angry about this lack of power!* He complains and blames others for each calamity instead of taking responsibility for his own life and utilizing the power he has. The Third Step reminds the depressive that he is now under the care of God, and he is then empowered to turn his back on the victim mentality.

The depressive will is unhealthily self-centered. If some action is not perceived as benefiting the self, the depressive usually finds some way to avoid it. Never mind that it would benefit another person in need—*me first* reigns supreme.

The depressive is not really good to himself, however. He constantly upbraids and scolds himself in his negative self-talk. Some depressives seem to prefer obsessing moodily on their own shortcomings, the evil and injustice in the world or some slight to their egos rather than do a constructive action that would benefit another human being.

With self-pity and self-centeredness running riot, the depressive will accumulate much resentment, envy, rancor, and self-loathing, which he then "gunnysacks" until it explodes in a major depression episode. ("Gunnysacking" is a term used by psychologists to describe the human tendency to stuff certain emotions into the unconscious without dealing with them.)

In contrast, the recovering person whose will and life has been entrusted to the care of God experiences a peace and joy never known before. Instead of self-pity, he concentrates on gratitude for the blessings he has received from God. By the daily discipline of writing down ten things for which he is grateful, he begins to change from seeing the glass of his life as one-half empty to one-half full.

Instead of playing the victim, the recovering depressive can take a proactive stance in life empowered and directed by God. He is no longer a victim. The creator of the universe loves him and is willing to assist him in the overcoming the trials of life.

Instead of incessant self-centered ruminations and self-recriminations, the recovering person can turn a deaf ear to the negative self-talk engendered by his depression-prone mind. If he *does* happen to listen to the negative self-talk, he disputes the negativity in the light of his new relationship with God. He reminds himself that he has now turned his will and his life over to the care of God. The negative self-talk is not of God and must be totally rejected.

One final note about this step: Many people develop intense fears when they feel they are supposed to turn their will and their life over to the care of God. Jane, a D.A. member, put is this way: "What if God tells me to go to Timbuktu as a missionary? What if God tells me to give away all my money to the poor? What if God tells me to go to a convent?"

Fortunately, anyone who has observed the workings of God can testify that the people God calls to go to Timbuktu are invariably happy and eager to go. St. Francis of Assisi, who was called to give his money to the poor, was glad to do so. People who are called to go to a monastery or convent are regularly seen to be joyful about this decision. The point is that if God calls a person to a particular occupation or section of the country, the usual method is to awaken in the person a *desire* to make the change.

God desires a person to be happy, joyous, and free. When God wants a person to make a drastic change in his life, God also supplies the willingness to make the change. Therefore, my answer to the question posed by Jane: "If the idea of going as a missionary to Timbuktu is horribly repulsive to you, that's probably a good sign that God *is not* and will not be calling you to do this."

MEMBERS SHARE THEIR
EXPERIENCES WITH THIS STEP

Turning my will and my life over to the care of God as I understood Him was one of the most liberating experiences of my life. Since I had struggled on and off with severe depression for at least thirty years, I knew that my life under *my* control was not happy, joyous, or free. The promises in the twelve-step programs caught my interest. What did I really have to lose by giving up my own will? Was I really that deliriously happy with the way I was running my own life? The answer was *no!*

I have found happiness and freedom now in turning my life over to the care of God. Each morning I make a fresh commitment: "God, this is your day. May your love flow to me and to others today." I no longer get so "bent out of shape" if unexpected events mess up the day. I remind myself that this is God's day, and He can help me pick up the pieces. And He does!

This surrender of my will to God reminds me of the experience of my friend, Amy. She owned an old car that was continually giving her trouble; it would either refuse to start or break down on the freeway as she was going to work. Amy was ready to have the car hauled away to the junkyard when her older brother spoke up.

"Amy, give the car to me. I've studied auto mechanics, and I believe I can get the car working. I'll drive you to work every day since I regularly go right by your office."

Amy's brother was able to fix the car, and her problems were solved. Likewise, our problems begin to dissolve when we take the Third Step.

Another benefit to the Third Step for me is that I am finally beginning to be honest with myself about what I am feeling. I had known for a long time that one of the reasons people get depressed is that they are cut off from their true feelings. Early in life, the depressive learns that his genuine feelings are to be avoided: his real feelings cause his parents to punish him, his real feelings get him in trouble with siblings and friends, his real feelings are shamed. He becomes quite skillful in hiding his true feelings from himself; they are anesthetized. He can then have all *nice, pretend* feelings.

The problem is that the real feelings are buried *alive*. If I refuse to recognize them, they will return to haunt me in the form of intense anxiety, obsessions, or depressions. I had known this for a long time, but I still found it difficult to get in touch with my authentic feelings. Some of them seemed to almost overwhelm me whenever I caught a glimpse of them.

The Third Step gave me a safety net. If my will and my life were under the care of an all-powerful God, He would surely not let me do something stupid and permanently destructive under the sway of my real feelings. If I asked God, He would not let my anger overwhelm me to the point that I injured someone else in word or behavior; likewise, He would not allow my sexual instincts to so overcome me that I behaved in a way I would later regret. I had a resource in living that I had not had before the Third Step.

QUESTIONS TO ASK MYSELF ABOUT
THE THIRD STEP

- What is preventing me from turning my will and my life over to the care of God?
- Am I inclined to self-pity? What can I do to stop being this way?
- Do I see myself as a victim in life? What steps can I take to get out of the victim stance?
- Am I willing to commit to writing a gratitude list each day?

- Do I ever do something just because it will help another person—-without calculating how I will benefit?
- Am I honest with myself about my real feelings?
- Am I willing to look more closely at myself and my life?

— NOTES —

Step Four

> **"Made a searching and fearless moral inventory of ourselves."**

This step needs to be written out by the member in preparation to be read to another human being (Step Five). Inventories are routine and essential for a successful business; a successful life can do no less. However, the depression-prone person is wise not to do this step when he is down. He will tend to be too hard on himself and ignore his strengths.

The fourth step is not a vehicle for self-hatred or vitriolic self-criticism. It should be conducted with a loving spirit toward the self and others. The member should be sure to include all his character assets as well as his character liabilities. When the member realizes that it is his buried resentments together with his fears and intense negativity that are primarily causing his pain, he will be powerfully motivated to deal with all this in a healthier manner.

One member, Jane*, argued with this idea: "All human beings have resentments and negativity; it's human. I know people who are much worse than I am, and they seem to be happy enough. They don't get depressed."

This is like the alcoholic saying that all his friends are able to take one alcoholic drink and stop. Since the alcoholic is unable to do this, he complains that it is not *fair* that he can't drink like his friends. Healing for the alcoholic comes when he stops protesting the unfairness and accepts the reality that *he* cannot take a drink without setting in motion a vicious cycle of drunkenness.

Similarly, the depressive learns to view resentments; they must be rooted out and dealt with if he is to find a joyful, happy life. Admittedly, this is not easy. Taking a first drink is simple to identify——you either do or you don't. Resentments are sneaky, elusive things. You must be constantly on guard for them. The rewards, however, are more than worth it.

Like A.A., this program only works if members are willing to be rigorously honest. As the A.A. big book states, "Rarely have we seen a person fail who has thoroughly followed our path. Those who do not recover are people . . . who are constitutionally incapable of being honest with themselves."[1]

In honesty, then, we begin writing down our character assets and liabilities. If we begin with our resentments in our liabilities section, we need to be thorough about all the people, places and things that irritate, displease or exasperate us. (Acknowledge that fear, distrust, and suspicion frequently are setups for resentment, so also write down what you suspect, fear, or distrust.)

A plan that has worked for some members is to write down every person, place, or thing that engenders resentment. Then, write down how you intend to cope with each situation——either by acceptance and forgiveness or by some concrete action to change the situation. Another alternative is to use a chart similar to the following:

Person, place or thing I resent	Why I resent this	Part of my life impacted by this

Some people find it difficult to get rid of hard feelings because they feel justified holding on to them. Amy, a high school science teacher involved in an abusive relationship, once remarked in a meeting, "John really did lie to me; he cheated on me; he verbally abused me at every opportunity. He doesn't deserve my forgiveness."

This attitude misses the point. Amy deserves the peace of mind that forgiveness will bring. Failure to forgive John and holding on to the resentment against him forms a block in Amy's life. The prayer we say at the close of each meeting states, "forgive us our trespasses *as we forgive those who trespass against us.*" An unsurrendered resentment blocks God's power and our own.

The depression-prone person frequently finds he has a profound resentment against himself. His self-talk is often a constant barrage of name calling, self-berating—lacerating the self about real or imagined misbehavior.

A prominent psychologist offers many suggestions for stopping this negative self-talk (which he calls rumination). He suggests ringing a bell, carrying a three-by-five card with the word STOP in large red letters or wearing a rubber band around the wrist and snapping it hard to stop the ruminating.[2]

Another helpful strategy in dealing with negative thoughts was suggested by a member in a D.A. meeting: "I like to use the analogy of an air-traffic controller," she said. "The controller decides which planes are allowed to land on the runway. In my life, I must be a thought-traffic controller. Many of my thoughts must be turned away and not allowed to land if I am to stay healthy and happy."

Also, the depressive has frequently allowed himself to be mistreated by other people in his life. (Because of his low self-esteem, he often feels he *deserves* to be mistreated.) At the deepest level of his being, the depressive needs to believe he deserves to be treated with dignity and respect. Like most people, he probably subscribes to the belief that all people are to be treated with dignity and respect. He needs to include himself in the all.

If there is someone in his life who constantly berates him and mistreats him, he owes it to himself to call for a change. This should be part of his inventory.

The inventory can take other forms, also. One very simple form is to fold a paper in half and list on the left side all of your character assets; on the right side, list all your character defects and liabilities.

For those who desire to do an intensive fourth step, both A.A. and Al-Anon have excellent literature that can guide in making an intensive fourth step.

There is an Appendix in the back of this book that explains some of the basic concepts of cognitive-behavioral therapy (CBT). CBT was started by Aaron Beck of the University of Pennsylvania in the 1970s and is now widely used. Beck's theory is that "one's thoughts about oneself are frequently destructive, and that by forcing the mind to think in certain ways one can actually change one's reality."[3] Thus, Beck has found that changing depressive thinking results in changing depressive feeling.

Studies have been made in an effort to determine which is more effective—antidepressant drug therapy or cognitive therapy. In at least one study, cognitive therapy was shown to be superior in results to antidepressant drug therapy.[4] Therefore, depressives should know some of the basic concepts of cognitive therapy and incorporate them in their fourth-step work.

MEMBERS SHARE THEIR
EXPERIENCES WITH THIS STEP

At first, I was reluctant to take an inventory of myself. It felt better to buy into the idea that all I had to do was take the right pill, and everything would be all right. Gradually, I began to see the truth that if I was continuing to go through periods of depression—

something was amiss in my physical, mental or spiritual life.

I realized that I needed to ask for God's guidance in ferreting out exactly what was behind all this depression. I would certainly not continue day after day taking aspirin if I had a toothache or a stomachache. I would go to the dentist or the doctor to find out what was causing the pain.

Depression is more elusive than toothaches or stomachaches, but I discovered there are things I can do to alleviate it. I started with the physical. I had not been exercising every day. Many studies have shown that physical exercise relieves depression. I resolved to start walking at least thirty minutes every day. I also decided to amend my diet to include more fruits, vegetables, and whole grains.

In regard to mental and spiritual health, I began the fourth step inventory. In examining my life closely, I saw few overt sins——the kind that would put me in trouble with the law. I had never killed anyone, stolen anything from a store, lied under oath, etc.

When I came to the resentment list, however, the list seemed to go on and on. I studied some of the principles of cognitive therapy to shed light on my problems. I was guilty of almost all the cognitive distortions—thinking errors that lead to depression. In myself, I could see that these distortions sprang from a basic resentment against God because my life was not going the way I wanted. This resentment had hardened into a persistent negativity that made me guilty of every thinking error on the list.

What was the root of all this negativity about God, about life? One of the roots I began to see was envy.

I examined all the encroachments of envy in my life and prayed to eradicate each. I realized that I was envious of women younger and prettier than I. I was

envious of people with more money. I was envious of
people who were more intelligent, more artistic, and
more energetic. Laughable! Ridiculous! I could find
something to envy in just about every person or situation.

Looking around at our culture, I began to see where
some of this envy originated. Our media advertising is
driven by the urge to incite envy in order to sell prod-
ucts. I had swallowed the bait and was hooked.

In the process of getting "unhooked," I reminded
myself that God had created me as I was with my looks,
my intelligence, and my talents. God didn't expect me
to surpass the others around me. I only needed to be my
best self, and He would assist me in doing that. There is
no place for envy!

Another thing I began to see was that I had always
felt superior to people who committed overt crimes like
murder, adultery, theft, and the like. I began to see that
my bitter attitude, unforgiving spirit and pettiness are
equally offensive to God.

I was reminded of a story told me by Jane, a single
mother of two. She had recently given a lavish party for
her two children because she had received an unexpected bonus at work. The daughter, Sue, was going
through a typical teenage blue funk and sat in a corner
during the entire party with a bored, sad look on her
face. Jane's son, Brian, thoroughly enjoyed the party
although he did pick a fight with one of the kids there,
poured Coke down one girl's back, and gobbled up half
of the shrimp himself. So, they ran out of shrimp. Em-
barrassing!

Jane told me that both children really disappointed
her, but Sue's attitude hurt her the most. Although she
disapproved of many of the things Brian had done, she
knew that he enjoyed the party and was grateful to her
for giving it. Sue was something else.

I had been like Sue in the party of life. God had given me this amazing gift of life, and I had spent most of my time in life complaining about the conditions and my lot instead of enjoying the feast before me.

Also in my fourth step inventory, I became aware that it is still very difficult for me to own up to my true feelings. My real feelings are rarely admirable; they are usually selfish, envious, or downright petty. I keep wanting to deny the truth, but healing comes only in facing the truth.

QUESTIONS TO ASK MYSELF ABOUT
THE FOURTH STEP

- Am I willing to begin writing this step today?
- What do "searching" and "fearless" mean to me?
- Am I honest in my dealings with myself and others?
- What comes to my mind when I hear the phrase "moral inventory"?

---

* In the discussion of the Twelve Steps, all first names have been changed to protect anonymity.

1 *Alcoholics Anonymous* (New York: Alcoholics Anonymous World Services, Inc., 2001) p. 58.

2 Martin E. P. Seligman, Ph.D., *Learned Optimism* (New York: Alfred A. Knopf, 1991) p. 218.

3 Andrew Solomon, *The Noonday Demon: An Atlas of Depression* (New York: Scribner, 2001) p. 107.

4 David D. Burns, *Feeling Good: The New Mood Therapy* (New York: New American Library, 1980) pp. 13-16.

— Notes —

STEP FIVE

> "Admitted to God, to ourselves, and to another human being the exact nature of our wrongs."

We have completed the Step Four inventory of ourselves. Consequently, we have already done part of Step Five; we have admitted to ourselves the exact nature of our wrongs. Now, we need to admit our wrongs to God and to another human being. Hopefully, we have come to understand God as loving, compassionate and nonjudgmental. This prepares the way for admitting our wrongs to another human being.

Note that there is nothing stated or implied in the Fifth Step about beating ourselves up with guilt for our wrongs. This is never productive. We face our wrongs squarely and honestly; for the present, this is sufficient.

We must choose the "another human being" with great care. We need someone who is not intimately connected to us and our situation. Many members choose their sponsors; others choose a clergyman, professional counselor or friend. The ideal person is one who will help us to see patterns in our behavior and not arbitrarily hand out advice.

After we select the person, we need to set a time and place to share our inventory. This could be at a quiet restaurant, someone's home, or a park. The important thing is that we set a date and specific time to meet with the person.

If we look closely at the Fifth Step, we realize that it is based on ancient principles. The Bible instructs us, "So then, confess your sins to one another"[1] and also, "But if we confess our sins to God . . . he will forgive us our sins. . . ."[2] Roman Catholics regularly go to a priest for confession.

In this step, we are seeking to know ourselves more fully by examining our deeds and the reasons for them. Our confidante is sometimes able to help us see the exact nature of our wrongs and the reasons behind them. When we have completed the Fifth Step, we have learned more about our actions and ourselves.

Some psychologists assert that we are only as sick as our secrets. Since this step requires us to tell our secrets to another human being, members frequently remark about the freedom and release they feel after talking with another person. Counselors report that many patients recover when they gain the courage to reveal a painful memory.

This step has another purpose: we begin to feel that *we* can be forgiven, no matter what we have done. When we feel forgiven by God, we can more easily forgive others.

Perhaps the largest bonus from Step Five is the relief from our feelings of isolation. Depressives tend to be loners who feel that no one else understands the pain they are experiencing. An A.A. publication expresses well the feeling of aloneness:

> Nearly all of us suffered the feeling that we didn't quite belong. Either we were shy, and dared not draw near others, or we were apt to be noisy good fellows craving attention and companionship, but never getting it—at least to our way of thinking. There was always that mysterious barrier we could neither surmount nor understand. It was as if we were actors on a stage, suddenly realizing that we did not know a single line of our parts.[3]

Coming out of our isolation into a dynamic relationship with another human being and with God produces healing and relief. The guilt we had stockpiled starts to dissipate.

The last phrase of the step "the exact nature of our wrongs" is important as well. A vague confession to God "forgive me for my sins" is a little like shooting an arrow at the sun as opposed to shooting at a bull's eye. When you have a specific target, you can focus your energies.

A popular psychologist expresses this same idea in a chapter of his book entitled, "You Can't Change What You Don't Acknowledge":

> I have long believed that 50 percent of the solution to any problem lies in defining the problem. Once you've had the courage and commitment to lay it out to yourself exactly as it is, then you cannot and will not spend another day in a fantasy.[4]

Although this step is difficult, it is essential to the healing we so desperately crave.

MEMBERS SHARE THEIR
EXPERIENCES WITH THIS STEP

For my Fifth Step, I decided that the other human being would be Betty Totten, the therapist I had been seeing off and on for about ten years. She already knew some of the dark areas of my life I had managed to keep hidden from others: the fact that when I was single I had had sexual affairs, that I had been bulimic for fifteen years earlier and stopped only when I realized the severe health dangers, that I had two failed marriages for which she helped me to realize I was fifty percent responsible.

She also knew little petty things about me: that I resented having the sole responsibility of caring for my aged mother, that even though I was a teacher, I really didn't like children all that much. She had known all these (to me) *shocking, despicable* things for quite a while and still treated me as though I were a valuable human being. I felt I could risk more honesty with her.

She did point out patterns in my thoughts and behavior: one example—the perfectionist patterns that really worked against me. Many times I had the attitude that if I couldn't do something perfectly, I wouldn't do it at all. I had cut myself out of a number of satisfying experiences because of this attitude. Also, this caused me to spend way too much time on some unimportant details because I felt that *everything* had to be perfect.

She helped me see that I was caught up in the victim stance. When things didn't go my way, I tended to withdraw into a corner, muttering to God, "Life is so unfair" and laying tons of angry logs on the resentment fire inside of me. I was doing all this as a kind of reflex action of which I was barely aware. But it was killing me with depression.

She deftly communicated that I was intensely self-centered—probably because I was raised as an only child in a relatively affluent home where little was denied me. I expected—no, I *demanded* that life continue to treat me as first class. Of course, this didn't happen, and I responded with a violent inner rage.

She also reconnected me with my Higher Power (whom I call God). When I first began seeing her, I had turned against God. If God were all powerful, why didn't He take away my depression? I was intensely angry about being afflicted with depression. I put the main blame on God, and since I didn't observe that God was instantly healing my depression, I had decided to dispense with God. I still believed in psychology and the ability of therapists to confront depression. That was why I had come to her in the first place.

I remember when Betty began mentioning God, I was taken aback. I didn't want to hear about God. God had betrayed me and deserted me. I had come to Betty because of her psychological know-how. I didn't want her reconnecting me with God. No, thank you very much.

But somehow, it happened. Betty is such a devoted Christian herself; her Christianity wasn't like a garment she could take off because it offended me. And it did offend me, but I kept seeing her because I began to realize that I was getting better. I couldn't accept her psychological help without somewhere deep inside acknowledging God as well.

I really don't know how it happened, but I became linked to God again. I can't point to any one blinding, Damascus Road experience, but I gradually became open to readmitting God into my life. Step Three became a reality for me, and the real healing began. I had chosen the right person for my Fifth Step.

QUESTIONS TO ASK MYSELF
ABOUT THE FIFTH STEP

- How do I feel about sharing all of my Fourth Step with another human being?
- Am I uneasy about admitting my faults to my Higher Power? Why?
- Can I accept that I am not perfect? Do I see how I have been harmed by constantly obsessing about perfection?
- What in my Fourth Step is most difficult to share with another human being? With whom would I feel most comfortable sharing this?
- Is there something I have left out of my Fourth Step because I feel, "This is something I could *never* tell anyone"? Examine this closely. This could be the crux of the pain!

— NOTES —

[1] *Good News Bible: Today's English Version* (New York: American
     Bible Society, 1978) James 5:16, p. 226.
[2] Ibid., 1 John 1:9, p. 234.
[3] *Twelve Steps and Twelve Traditions* (New York: Alcoholics Anony-
     mous World Services, Inc., 1994) p. 57.
[4] Phillip C. McGraw, Ph.D., *Life Strategies* (New York: Hyperion,
     1999) p. 123.

STEP SIX

"Were entirely ready to have God remove all these defects of character."

This step is a continuation of the Third Step. Many people can turn their will and their life over to the care of God in a global way, but they face real difficulty bringing God into their character defects.

Removing character defects is inevitably a slow process. Not many cases of instant character transformation are recorded. True, the hopeless alcoholic is often delivered from his compulsion to drink; the addict is sometimes dramatically freed from his addiction. But then, the real work begins—the ongoing growth work in becoming more loving, less greedy, more peaceable.

Here a serious problem arises—do we *really* want all our character defects removed? We acknowledge that God wants to remove them, but what about us? What about the character defects that we enjoy? Are we willing to give up the pride we sometimes feel when we note our superiority to another person? Are we willing to give up lust in a society that tempts us at every turn? Are we willing to give up gossip? What about gluttony and envy? (Our advertising systems are built around generating envy. Are we even able to resist being envious?) Are we willing to give up even a part of our selfishness?

The requirements of this step are apt to make some of us exclaim like the veteran churchgoer: "When the preacher preaches against drunkenness, adultery and murder, I call that real preaching. When he starts railing against gluttony, sloth and greed, I call that meddling."

The idea here is to be ready to have God make a transformation in our lives—be *ready* to be a more loving, unselfish person, be *ready* to be made less greedy,

43

less dependent on money and power, be *ready* to let go
of all our resentments. Readiness is all that this step
requires.

In being ready to have our character defects removed, it is helpful to identify precisely what they are.
A good place for the depressive to start is with the
character defects that are fueling his depression, the
source of most of his pain. Each person is different, and
God will reveal to each person the specific flaws he
needs to address. Nevertheless, there are qualities that
almost all depressives have in common. It is helpful to
be aware of these.

One of these defects is a tendency to hold on to
resentments and ruminate about them. When we find
ourselves resistant to giving up a resentment, we need
to ask ourselves, "What's the payoff for holding on to
this unforgiving spirit?" A popular Al-Anon book speaks
to this matter:

> Lately, I've been struggling with forgiveness.
> If I remain unforgiving, the payoff is that I can
> savor thoughts of revenge. I can feel sorry for
> myself for the hurt that was inflicted on me. I can
> justify my actions and remain distant. I don't have
> to work toward a closer relationship with that
> person if I remain unforgiving.[1]

Another characteristic fault of the depressive personality is the tendency to deny and repress feelings. An
eminent psychologist comments on this fault:

> Now, people with depression hardly let them-
> selves feel any emotion at all. Instead of the nor-
> mal fluctuations of happiness, sadness, disap-
> pointment, joy, desire, and anger that most people
> cycle through many times a day, depressed people
> feel a kind of gray neutrality."[2]

He goes on to comment that depressives still feel guilt about their emotions even though they don't allow themselves to experience them.

The implication of all this is that the depressive needs to be willing to experience his emotions—good and bad. The depressive is afraid of his negative emotions, especially anger. When he develops the trust that his Higher Power will provide the wisdom to deal appropriately with his anger and other negative emotions, he becomes willing to experience the emotions directly.

In addition to a willingness to experience his true feelings, the depressive needs a readiness to become more unselfish. A famous psychologist who has devoted many years to studying depression comments:

> Depression, I have argued, stems partly from an overcommitment to the self and an under-commitment to the common good. This state of affairs is hazardous to our health. . . . The sacrifice involved in giving to others and spending serious time, money, and effort enhancing the common good does not come naturally to the present generation.[3]

He goes on to suggest that healing will come for the depressive when he commits to helping his fellow man. We will deal with this more extensively in Step Twelve, but the readiness to be more unselfish should begin now.

MEMBERS SHARE THEIR EXPERIENCES WITH THIS STEP

When I began this Sixth Step, I asked myself if I were truly ready to have God remove my character defects. When I made the connection between my character defects and the pain of depression, the willingness came.

I frequently ask myself this question: Do I want to hold on to this resentment, unforgiving spirit, selfish outlook, etc. or do I want to be happy, joyous and free? I remind myself that I cannot have both.

When I began examining my life in light of the character flaws shared by most depressives, I started with resentments. Am I willing to give up present and future resentments? Again, connecting my resentments to the intense pain I had felt in depression resulted in readiness to give them up.

In the Fourth Step, I felt I had gotten rid of the resentments in my past, but I find little resentments cropping up every day. For example, I was sitting in church yesterday and found myself becoming intensely angry at some young children behind me who were whispering to each other. Driving home, a guy in the car behind me honked his horn because I was moving too slowly for him—I found myself muttering obscenities. Next I went to the grocery store to pick up a few things for lunch; when I saw the long line, my resentment meter started rising.

It's an ongoing job, this monitoring of resentments! It reminds me of my ongoing job of monitoring my intake of monosodium glutamate (MSG). About ten years ago, I discovered that I could not tolerate foods containing MSG without developing a headache. Now I carefully read labels on foods and refuse to ingest anything with MSG. The result—-no more headaches![4]

The character fault of denying feelings really speaks to me. I have resolved each day to face and experience my real feelings. This is often very painful for me. Only very rarely do my true feelings reflect anything noble or unselfish, but nevertheless I am committed to being rigorously honest with myself about my feelings.

In regard to the readiness to become more unselfish, here is where I really fall short. For almost everything I do, a selfish motive can be found at the core. I do nice things for my friends; they will probably do something nice for me one day. I do a good deed to help my family; they will assist me when I need help. On and on it goes.

I decided to start some giving in my life wherein the expectation of return was slim or none. I decided to bring some food and offer rides to three or four people I knew who would probably never be in a position to return the favor. I would pledge some money to my church. I would look for more opportunities where I could genuinely help another person in need (without the expectation that person might be in a position to help me later on). I would look only at whether I could be of real assistance to them.

I truly became ready to have God remove all my defects of character because I was beginning to see how these character defects opened the door to my depressions.

QUESTIONS TO ASK MYSELF ABOUT THE SIXTH STEP

- Who in my life is most difficult to forgive?
- Am I willing to give up gossip? gluttony? greed?
- Am I willing to give up my feelings of superiority or of inferiority?
- Am I ready to become more unselfish?
- Do I have the courage to face my real feelings?

— Notes —

---

[1] *Paths to Recovery* (Virginia Beach, VA: Al-Anon Family Groups, 1997) p. 68.

[2] Richard O'Connor, Ph.D., *Undoing Depression: What Therapy Doesn't Teach You and Medication Can't Give You* (New York: Little, Brown and Company, 1997; Berkley Books, 1999) p. 98.

[3] Martin E.P. Seligman, Ph.D., *Learned Optimism* (New York: Simon & Schuster Inc., 1998) p. 288.

[4] Later I was reading a book about losing weight that advised all people trying to control their weight to avoid MSG. The book stated that MSG was the chemical fed to laboratory rats when scientists were trying to get them to gain weight. I'm glad now that I'm allergic to MSG because it's something I shouldn't be eating anyway.

Step Seven

> **"Humbly asked Him to remove our short-comings."**

We will note a natural progression in the steps. In Step Four, we *identified* our shortcomings. In Step Six we became *ready* to have God remove them. In this step, we ask Him in humility to *remove* them.

"Humbly" is the first word in this step. By this word we acknowledge that by our own power we cannot get rid of our shortcomings. At the same time, confident that we have the help of our Higher Power, we must begin to take some action. "Sitting back and behaving in all the same old ways while asking God to remove the defects is not effective. We cannot continue to do the same things over and over and expect different results."[1]

This step then is a call to action on our part. "Pray as though it all depends on God; work as though it all depends on you" is a phrase that expresses this paradox well. We begin here to make some changes in our thoughts and behavior assured that God is guiding and assisting us.

While each person's character flaws are different, there are certain ones shared by most depressives. Many have been pointed out at various points throughout the discussion of Steps One through Six. Now it is helpful to group these defects all together. Any soldier going into battle needs to be able to clearly identify his enemy; this list identifies some of our major enemies:

The depressive has a tendency:
  1) to engage in negative self-talk

2)   to be a pessimist
3)   to be a perfectionist
4)   to hoard resentments
5)   to deny authentic feelings
6)   to lack balance in attending to the needs of self
      and others
7)   to isolate from people
8)   to be a doormat and a victim
9)   to tolerate stress poorly
10)   to experience difficulty making decisions

The above list can alert us to the changes we need to begin making. These ten (especially the first four) react together in a synergistic way; that is, all together they produce a more damaging effect than if they each occurred in isolation.

Following are some suggestions for overcoming these faults:

1) **Disposition to negative self-talk.** Looking closely at the negative self-talk, we find that it is comprised of many irrational and erroneous statements. It is important to challenge these statements. The slogan "Don't believe everything you think" applies here. Step Four also contains helpful suggestions for dealing with negative self-talk.

2) **Persistent pessimistic orientation toward life.** For suggestions about changing from the pessimist stance, see Appendix B—*Learned Optimism*. The simple reminder that our Higher Power, the creator and sustainer of the universe, is by our side assisting and sustaining us often deflates pessimism. If we keep this truth in our minds, there is no room for pessimism.

3) **Temperament prone to perfectionism.** There are many ways to cease being a perfectionist. One is by

reminding ourselves that relentlessly pursuing perfection is chasing a mirage:

"Perfection" is man's ultimate illusion. It simply doesn't exist in the universe. There is no perfection. It's really the world's greatest con game; it promises riches and delivers misery.[2]

Another insight in fighting perfectionism is the realization that it is fueled by fear:

You may not be aware that fear always lurks behind perfectionism. Fear is the fuel that drives your compulsion to polish things to the ultimate. If you choose to give up your perfectionism, you may initially have to confront this fear.[3]

4) **Tendency to hoard resentments.** This follows logically from the previous discussions. If a person is relentlessly pursuing perfection, he is bound to accumulate resentments. If his basic attitude toward life is pessimistic, the resentments increase exponentially. Furthermore, the depressive tends to ruminate about his resentments and resists giving them up. This implants the negative feelings more firmly in the mind.

So many destructive attitudes cluster around resentment; many people feel that this is the most damaging of the ten defects.

One way the depressive adds to his stockpile of resentments is through his feeling of entitlement. He feels *entitled* to happiness without any effort or struggle on his part. Therefore, when he experiences sadness of any sort, he goes immediately to anger and indignation.

The next step is usually blaming someone or something for his gloom. He will blame his spouse, his children, his employer, himself or God. All this creates a vicious cycle that spirals down to deep depression. The thought process goes something like this:

"I feel miserable."

"That's not right! I'm entitled to happiness."

"It's _____'s fault; _____ is to blame."

"I hate _____."

I continue to think and stew about all of _____'s injustices to me.

If instead of useless blaming, he begins to take responsibility for his unhappiness and starts making some changes in his thoughts and behavior, he will be on the road to recovery.

5) **Inclination to deny authentic feelings and be out of touch with real emotion.** This is again a call to awareness. The depressive must be blatantly honest with himself and continually ask, "What am I *really feeling* in this situation?" He will remind himself that he is not to judge his feelings and not impulsively act on his feelings. Just to be aware of the truth about his emotions is an important step in the right direction.[4]

This flaw helps to explain why the depressive seems unable to deal with the ordinary losses and problems of life. Unaware of his authentic emotions, the depressive cannot process the life losses he experiences. He is like a blindfolded man trying to make his way through a busy city.

6) **Tendency to be out of balance in attending to the needs of self and others.** Either the depressive neurotically neglects his own needs and obsessively focuses on the concerns of others, or he blocks out everyone else and is completely self-absorbed. The healthy person takes care of both his own needs and focuses energy on helping others. Step Twelve and Appendix B addresses this in more detail.

7) **Proneness to isolate from others and withdraw into the self.** This isolation tendency is one of the reasons why belonging to a Depression Anonymous group

and attending meetings regularly are so beneficial to the depressive.

Advice to depressives to counteract this tendency to isolate: force yourself to go to social gatherings you formerly enjoyed—even though you don't *feel* like going. Call friends on the telephone. Get a list of everyone's phone number in your Depression Anonymous group, and call them when you feel lonely and isolated.

8) **Inclination to be a doormat and a victim**. Those with a doormat disposition find themselves disrespected and often abused by others. They are usually "people pleasers" who don't stand up for themselves. Assertiveness training courses can be of great benefit; many private psychologists, community centers, and mental health clinics offer these courses. Learning healthy assertiveness will also help shake the depressive out of the victim stance.

The victim stance is closely related to that of the doormat. The person playing the victim may have been truly hurt by someone in the past, but instead of putting it behind him and moving on, he gets trapped in the hurt. "Feeling victimized usually feels comforting at first. It's a sanctuary of self-involvement. It paves the path to indulgence and creates community with other victims. But it kills you with kindness. You . . . begin to enjoy it."[5]

How then does a person stop feeling like a victim? "If you sincerely love yourself and are truly proud of what you are, it becomes very difficult to feel like a victim."[6] You put the past behind you and move on.

9) **Low tolerance for stress.** Knowing that added stress is a trigger for depression should make the depressive proactive in eliminating all the stressors he can. He can leave early for appointments, so he avoids the stress he feels if traffic delays or other unexpected

events intervene. He can look ahead and prepare for upcoming events so that frantic, last minute stresses are avoided. He can say "no" outright to certain stressors that he has been living with out of habit.

10) **Difficulty making decisions.** This is closely related to perfectionism. Feeling that he must make the *perfect* decision, he procrastinates and makes no decision.

The depressive can remind himself that endless ruminating is counter-productive. An imperfect decision is often better than no decision. He will learn from the bad decision; no decision freezes him and renders him paralyzed.

MEMBERS SHARE THEIR
EXPERIENCES WITH THIS STEP

I looked over the list of character flaws and saw that I was guilty of every one on the list. I decided to make some changes beginning with number Seven because I had already worked on numbers One through Six

When I am going through a depressed period, I definitely withdraw from other people. I decided to build more connections in my life. I felt that I had adequate friend, organizational, and family connections. I needed to give all of these continual maintenance, but I didn't necessarily need to expand my circle. What I needed was a more human relationship with the strangers I encountered regularly. I began to make a special effort to engage store clerks and other service personnel on a personal level instead of a mechanical, robotic level.

I started by giving honest compliments: "You're the fastest, most efficient checker I've ever had in this store." "You are really good at giving shots; that didn't hurt a bit." "You really know the merchandise in this store."

Even a simple comment about the weather establishes a small human link.

The doormat disposition was certainly another character defect. I came a long way in combating this flaw when I took a course called Assertive Discipline for Teachers about fifteen years ago. At that time, the course was a real lifesaver in terms of keeping my job as a high school English teacher. The class not only enabled me to keep my job and discipline the students, but it also had the side effect of making me a more assertive person, less inclined to be a doormat.

Concerning the low tolerance for stress, I remembered that when I was desperately depressed I would become completely unglued by an unexpected pressure. I learned then that in order to cope with life I needed to anticipate stressors and prepare in advance how to cope with them.

For example, since I was going to college at that time, exam time was a predictable stress. I decided to keep up with my studies each day so that when exam time came, it was a simple matter of reviewing.

Previously, I had waited until the day before the exam, stayed up all night writing a late paper, and crammed in all the information I could—only to become so incapacitated by panic, I fell apart. I learned that I couldn't put off important things to the last minute, or I would be completely overwhelmed and incapacitated.

I confronted my difficulty in making decisions; perfectionism was definitely operating here. I wanted to make the *perfect* decision every time. So, I often ended up in a state of utter terror and paralysis.

I developed a procedure: when I had an important decision to make, I would first write down in two columns the pro's and con's of the decision I was contemplating. I would pray for wisdom and (looking at the sheet before me) determine what appeared to be the wisest choice. Then, I would make the decision, repeating

to myself, "A bad decision is better than no decision." I
would then go on with my life and not look back.

QUESTIONS TO ASK MYSELF ABOUT
THE SEVENTH STEP

- Go through each character flaw and ask yourself,
  "Do I do this?" "How is this manifested in my life?"
- What do I feel is meant by humility? Do I know
  anyone who is humble?
- Can I think of a helpful slogan or phrase to repeat to
  myself that will assist my recovery?
- Am I beginning to see the changes I need to make as
  exciting challenges instead of dull drudgery?
- Am I developing the ability to laugh at some of my
  mistakes? Can I see how some of my past mistakes
  can benefit others?

— NOTES —

[1] *Paths to Recovery* (Virginia Beach, VA: Al-Anon Family Groups,
    1997) p. 73.
[2] David D. Burns, M.D., *Feeling Good: The New Mood Therapy* (New
    York: William Morrow and Co., Inc., 1980) p. 309-310.
[3] Ibid., p. 315.
[4] See Step Six discussion.
[5] Dan Baker, Ph.D. and Cameron Stauth, *What Happy People Know*
    (New York: St. Martin's Griffin, 2004) p. 159.
[6] Ibid., p. 163.

STEP EIGHT

> "Made a list of all persons we had harmed, and became willing to make amends to them all."

Steps Eight and Nine are concerned with our dealings with other people. They aim to clean up any past wreckage and clear the way for better future relationships.

One way to create the list is to write down the name of anyone who makes us feel uncomfortable or irritated: (1) Some names jump out; we sense we have harmed them in some way. (2) Others require careful searching to discover what makes us so uncomfortable. (3) A few are people who have harmed us; we have not really injured them. If we are harboring resentment against these people, however, we need to forgive them for our own peace of mind.

This brings us face to face with the necessity of forgiveness. We may think that some people don't warrant our forgiveness; we feel they wronged us without a cause. The point is that forgiveness is a gift we give to ourselves, not the other person. The burden of carrying around an unforgiving spirit is great indeed.

A.A. literature offers helpful insights into our difficulty with forgiveness:

> The moment we ponder a twisted or broken relationship with another person, our emotions go on the defensive. To escape looking at the wrongs we have done another, we resentfully focus on the wrong he has done us. This is especially true if he has, in fact, behaved badly at all. Triumphantly we seize upon his misbehavior as the perfect excuse for minimizing or forgetting our own.[1]

Scientists are beginning to find real value in forgiveness. Stanford University psychologist Carl Thoresen did a forgiveness study with 259 adults. The group members who were helped to forgive "saw stress, anger and symptoms such as headaches and stomach upsets go way down, compared with a control group." The positive effects continued for six months.[2]

Some members included on their list the people they had harmed because of things they *neglected* to do. They had been so paralyzed by depression that they were unable to do many necessary things.

For example, Amy, a single mother of two, realized that she had harmed her children because (in her severely depressed state) she was not able to give them the love and support they needed. She had been so immobilized by her own pain that she couldn't see the needs of others around her.

Frequently, the person prone to depression must make amends to himself in addition to other people. He has allowed himself to become a "doormat"; he has allowed another person to treat him badly. Whether he chooses to confront the situation head on or endure it, he must realize that he is a person of worth and value. He must not allow another person's poor opinion of him to affect the way he feels about himself. He will remind himself that it is God's opinion of him that matters.

A twelve-step group member shares why she decided to put herself on her list:

> I went to a Step Eight meeting and heard a woman share about putting herself at the top of her list. That idea hit home. How many times had I beaten myself for things that were not my fault? So I put myself on my Eighth Step list."[3]

Often members realize that they need to put God on their list. They had been intensely angry and resentful of

God, not trusting or following Him. They were in direct rebellion against God.

So now we have an amends list that includes other people and quite possibly ourselves and God. Is there anything further we need to do with Step Eight? One thing to consider is the problem of embarrassment. It was hard enough to admit our wrongs to another human being and God in the Fifth Step. Now the thought of writing or visiting the people on our amends list seems overwhelming. This is especially true when we feel that many on our list are still angry with us:

> There were cases, too, where we had damaged others who were still happily unaware of being hurt. Why, we cried, shouldn't bygones be by-gones? Why do we have to think of these people at all? These were some of the ways in which fear conspired with pride to hinder our making a list of *all* the people we had harmed."[4]

MEMBERS SHARE THEIR
EXPERIENCES WITH THIS STEP

In making my Eighth Step list, I couldn't in honesty overlook my two ex-husbands. True, I had expounded at length to relatives and friends about the failings of both men. I tried to give everyone the impression that I was the totally innocent one in both situations.

I had my stories down pat from telling them over and over. John, my first husband, had a quick temper. Since I was around him most of the time, I was the logical target of his anger. Unable to deal with his temper, I would shove down all my feelings and end up severely depressed. I became convinced that he was the cause of all my depression. I said to myself, "Get rid of him and be free of depression." So, I got on a plane and left him. (Sadly, the depression came back a year later.)

My second husband, Roy, had fallen in love with a woman twenty years younger then I. I desperately tried to keep the marriage together, but he insisted on a divorce. Nothing that I could say would dissuade him. I kept up my charade of being the totally innocent injured party for many years. When I began attending a twelve-step group regularly, I decided to look at my part in the two failed marriages.

Twelve-step literature consistently refuses to let a person blame others for the problems in life: "It is a spiritual axiom that every time we are disturbed, no matter what the cause, there is something wrong *with us*. If somebody hurts us and we are sore, we are in the wrong also."[5]

Gradually, I became able to see my part in the failure of both relationships. I discovered after the divorce that it was my *resentful reaction* to John's rage that was truly causing my depression. In addition, I realized how some of my faults had made Roy vulnerable to the other woman. I put both husbands on my amends list.

I then placed myself on the amends list. I had definitely been a doormat most of my life. The reasons for staying in the doormat mentality were varied: I was afraid that if I began asserting myself I would be disliked or punished. With husbands, I was afraid of being slapped, condemned or sued for divorce.

With friends, I was afraid that I would be ostracized and abandoned. I could see myself going out on a limb asserting myself, only to have the limb crash to the ground. Fear kept me in a state of inertia. I squelched my definite opinions when I was around friends for fear that if I expressed them, my friends might reject me.

God was definitely on my list. I knew down deep that God was in charge of this whole show called life. And since life was bringing me a great deal of pain, I placed the blame squarely on God. "Since you are all powerful, God, you could make me feel better." When I didn't feel better no matter how desperately I begged, my rage exploded inside.

QUESTIONS TO ASK MYSELF ABOUT
THE EIGHTH STEP

- Am I being rigorously honest with my list?
- Have I procrastinated about making my list? Why?
- Is there someone I feel I could never forgive? Do I see how this unforgiving spirit is harming me?
- Have I included myself on my list? God?

[1] *Twelve Steps and Twelve Traditions* (New York: Alcoholics Anonymous World Services, Inc., 1994) p. 78.
[2] Marilyn Elias, "To Err Is Human" *USA Today*, qtd. in *Readers Digest*, January 2002.
[3] *Paths to Recovery* (Virginia Beach, VA: Al-Anon Family Groups, 1997) p. 85.
[4] *Twelve*, p. 79.
[5] *Twelve*, p. 90.

— NOTES —

STEP NINE

"Made direct amends to such people wherever possible, except when to do so would injure them or others."

In Step Eight, we made a list of people we had harmed (and possibly included ourselves and God). Step Nine is a call to action.

In order to act, we need a plan. One plan is to start with the easy amends first. Another helpful approach is to divide the list into: (1) those people with whom we interact daily, (2) those who live in distant cities and (3) those deceased. It is also beneficial to list the type of amends we intend to make with each—direct confrontation, a letter, or changed behavior only.

An important distinction should be made between making amends and making an apology. An apology means expressing sorrow and regret for something we have done. An amends goes a step further and aims to correct or repair the harm done. In our amends, we state our realization of the harm we have done and how we intend to correct it. The other person may continue to be angry with us, but this should not dissuade us. His reaction is not our responsibility.

Never forget that our amends for things we have done in the past carries with it our resolve to act differently in the future. Nelly went to her next-door neighbor, Stephanie, and confessed that she had gossiped about her many times in the past. Nelly must cease her gossiping, or her amends are a sham.

The phrase in Step Nine that states "except when to do so would injure them or others" is a judgment call. One member offered this suggestion: "Check your

motives." You might discuss the proposed amends with
your sponsor or a friend to find additional insight:

> An example could be marital infidelity. While
> everyone involved may be knowledgeable of the
> situation, we have to consider whether or not our
> amends will open old wounds. We can start by
> replacing the neglect of our partner with loving,
> focused attention rather than imposing details that
> create further pain.[1]

At any rate, we need to be rigorously honest about
our amends. Are we nervous about causing the other
person pain or are we nervous about causing ourselves
pain by our admission of guilt? If the answer is the
latter, we need to remember that suppressing the urge
to make amends will only create more suffering for us in
the future.

Members are often confused about making amends
to people who have died. Some have written letters to
the deceased and read the letters at the grave. Another
method might be to behave in ways that would have
delighted the deceased: donate some money to their
church or favorite charity, give assistance to people or
animals they loved, and keep their memory alive in
various ways.

Many members struggle with procrastination in
making amends. We are creative in making excuses to
ourselves about how the time is not quite right at the
present to make the necessary amends. We must confront our evasion head on. "Just do it."

Many thoughts go through our minds at this point.
We imagine the other person thinking: "Why is he
bringing this up after all these years?" or "This letter is
weird—why is he writing to me?" or "It's about time
that S.O.B. realized all the harm done." Or, we say to

ourselves: "They'll think it was all totally my fault, and they will never acknowledge their part in the situation."

This last thought: whether or not the other person realizes his blame in the situation is really not our concern. Our only responsibility is to acknowledge our part. A good point to remember is:

> Above all, we should try to be absolutely sure that we are not delaying because we are afraid. For the readiness to take the full consequences of our past acts, and to take responsibility for the well being of others at the same time, is the very spirit of Step Nine.[2]

MEMBERS SHARE THEIR
EXPERIENCES WITH THIS STEP

In my Eighth Step, I had put my two ex-husbands on my list. I found myself procrastinating. I had decided to write letters to both, but it was about six months after my decision that I actually wrote both letters. One day, something inside me insisted—now is the time!

Dear John,

I know you must think it strange to get a letter from me. While I have blamed you many times for the failure of our relationship (in my own mind and my conversation), I have come to realize my own equal part in that failure.

To begin with, it is now clear to me that you did *not* cause my depression. I thought you did at the time; that was why I fled to Texas and went along quite happily with the divorce proceedings. I was getting rid of my depression by getting rid of you. Only one year later, the depression was back, so I had to face the fact that I had made a decision to react to you in a certain negative way. That I believe brought on the depression.

Specifically, I dealt with your anger in all the wrong ways. Instead of calmly negotiating a solution that would have benefited both of us, I "clammed up" when you were angry with me. I froze and began stuffing all my resentment inside. When you became angry with me, I was equally angry, but instead of energizing me to find a constructive solution, I stuffed it all inside and the result was terrible depression.

I now realize how painful it must have been to live with a person who was as severely depressed as I was (most of the time). That insight has only recently dawned on me. I was so caught up in my own pain that I never considered things from your point of view.

I now know that while I did love you deeply at one time, the accumulated resentment that I stuffed gradually turned that love into hatred. Instead of imploring God to change my feelings, I turned against God as well. Why would a good God allow me to go through the excruciating pain of depression? I felt God had failed me, so I turned my back on Him as well.

I know now that God has forgiven me and restored me to His fellowship, but I have been too proud until now to ask for your forgiveness.

He wrote back a week later that he appreciated my letter. "Of course, I forgive you," he graciously said. He realized that our relationship was on firm ground now; our friendly feelings were sure to positively impact our two children.

Then, I sent the following letter to my second husband, Roy:

Dear Roy,

I know you must think it strange to get a letter from me. While I have blamed you many times for the failure of our relationship (in my own mind and in my conversation), I have come to realize my own equal part in that failure.

To begin with, I now realize that it must have been painful to live with someone who was as depressed as I was (periodically). Depression makes a person moody and self-centered. That is not pleasant to live with.

Perhaps my greatest fault was my failure to love your daughter, Rhonda, and my active jealousy of her. I wanted you to love me more than you loved her. I saw the love you had for her as subtracting from the love you had for me. I now see how very wrong that was. Loving one person only enlarges our soul so that we may more truly love others, but I did not see that during the time I was married to you.

I can see now that if I had asked God to help me love and accept Rhonda, He would have done so. I did not do that. Instead, I built up a great deal of resentment against Rhonda in my mind, made a mental catalog of all her shortcomings and actively sought to make you love me more than her. I can now see how very evil that was. She was only a fourteen-year old kid! Of course, she had some faults, but I should have been the adult and shown her unconditional love.

I was also much too concerned about money —how I would fare in retirement and old age. I felt that all my problems would be solved if I just had enough money. I now see the foolishness of this attitude. I can also see how this and my attitude toward Rhonda caused you to fall out of love with me. If my behavior had been different, I don't think Kathy would have been that attractive to you.

I am grateful that God has forgiven me for all these sins. Until now, I have been too proud to ask for your forgiveness.

To date, I have not heard from him. I feel better, however, having written the letter.

My children were on my list because I realized that I had omitted doing many things for them because of my depressions. I told them both how I felt. In the last ten years, I have given emotional support and some financial support to both of them. My relationship with my children is now so very nourishing to me; I have two very dear adult friends in my children.

My amends to myself: I have resolved to amplify that barely audible whisper inside me, which I know now is the voice of my real feelings. I will listen to that weak voice and fight for it instead of automatically squelching it.

My amends to God: some may think it is rather presumptuous to state that I harmed God. How can a dust mite harm an elephant? The God of my understanding, however, is one who is grieved when I do not return His love; He chooses to be vulnerable to me. This is almost incomprehensible, but I believe it is true.

Such love prompts me to love in return. I have joined a church and pledge to the budget of the church. I pray regularly. I continue my third step each day with a conscious statement at the beginning of each day, "This is your day, God; I dedicate myself to you today. May your love touch me and other people today."

QUESTIONS TO ASK MYSELF ABOUT
THE NINTH STEP

- Do I understand the difference between making an apology and making amends?
- Do I want to write out what I intend to say to various people? Would that make the process easier?
- With which amends do I find myself procrastinating?
- In making amends to myself, what can I start doing today?

---

[1] *Paths to Recovery* (Virginia Beach, VA: Al-Anon Family Groups, 1997) p. 91.

[2] *Twelve Steps and Twelve Traditions* (New York: Alcoholics Anonymous World Services, Inc., 1994) p. 87.

— Notes —

STEP TEN

"Continued to take personal inventory and when we were wrong promptly admitted it."

Someone has said of the political realm that "eternal vigilance is the price of freedom." Vigilance is also essential in the area of recovery. We have to be constantly on guard for the negative thoughts and behaviors that will escalate to depression.

Step Ten is a maintenance step. Although a person may thoroughly clean his house once a year, there is always the need for periodic dusting, vacuuming and straightening up. Likewise, recovery requires ongoing attention.

Twelve-step programs aren't the only ones emphasizing ongoing self-searching. A prominent psychotherapist offers this advice about recovery from depression:

> It requires a total commitment to change. It means accepting that much of what you take for granted about yourself contributes to your depression, and that you, and no one else, have to devote a lot of time and energy to a continuous self-examination. Then it means that you will have to self-consciously practice new skills to replace your old habits of depression.[1]

It's important that we not lose patience with ourselves because the same character flaws keep surfacing. One member complained, "I've dealt with my resentments so many times; I thought by now I'd have won the battle and would no longer have to fight feeling resentful."

Since we are human, there are certain faults that will continue to show up as long as we are alive. We acknowledge in the Tenth Step that just because we did an exhaustive Fourth Step, we are not set for life. Certain flaws gradually extinguish themselves; others will persist to our dying day. These shortcomings require routine maintenance and regular requests for God to assist us. We should expect this and not be surprised.

It's a little like driving a car that is out of alignment. Take your hands off the steering wheel, and the car tends to go to the left. You must consciously and constantly turn the wheel to the right if you expect to drive safely.

Being a depressive is much the same way; our enemy attitudes (in Step Seven) are constantly with us. We must consciously steer our lives away from them. It gets easier and easier, but few of us ever reach the stage of perfect alignment. We have to "continue to take personal inventory" and when we are veering to the left, take appropriate action.

Another reason we must continue to take personal inventory is that life is constantly changing. New people and situations are introduced into our life, and many of these can throw us off balance.

When we become aware that we are off balance and slipping into old thought patterns and behaviors, we need a quick intervention. This is not a call to beat ourselves up; recognition of our error and a resolve to correct it is sufficient.

There are many ways to approach this continuing inventory: (1) a minute-by-minute awareness that notes infractions on the spot, (2) a daily check-up at night before going to sleep, (3) a decision to do a Fourth Step each year on a specified month. It is helpful to commit to a plan.

It's also a good idea to examine the ten character flaws shared by most depressives (in Step Seven) and copy on a card the ones that apply to you. Put this card somewhere where you can see it often; it will remind you to get back on a healthy track.

The tendency to generate and hold on to resentments seems to be the character flaw that plagues most people on a continuing basis. A.A. literature offers advice that steers us toward compassion:

> Finally, we begin to see that all people, including ourselves, are to some extent emotionally ill as well as frequently wrong, and then we approach true tolerance and see what real love for our fellows actually means. It will become more and more evident as we go forward that it is pointless to become angry, or to get hurt by people who, like us, are suffering from the pains of growing up.[2]

MEMBERS SHARE THEIR
EXPERIENCES WITH THIS STEP

I had finally reached the point where I was in dead earnest about changing my character flaws, and I realized that it was a daily challenge. I decided to take the same hard line in my life against envy, resentment, and negative ruminations that I have done against stealing or killing.

When I walk into a store, I am not constantly tempted to pocket something and run off with it. When someone offends me, I do not struggle with a desire to get a gun and "blow the guy away." Long ago, I made a decision that stealing from stores and shooting someone were absolutely out of the question. They never entered my mind as possibilities.

Something of this hard-line approach is needed for me in the encroachments of resentment, envy, and negative self-talk. A part of my mind argues: "Everyone struggles with these things. A little resentment and envy are nothing to be concerned about."

I then remind myself that indeed for me they do merit concern. Perhaps others can tolerate large amounts of resentment, envy, and negative self-talk, but allowed to stay in my life these temptations will turn to depression. They are similar to severe allergens. The average person can be around cats, dogs, pollen, and dust and suffer no ill effects. But to the severely allergic, these things cause sniffling, sneezing, drippy noses, and (sometimes) life-threatening symptoms.

I am severely allergic to resentment, envy, and negative self-talk. If I eliminate these from my life with the same zeal as if they were dangerous allergens, I know my depression will be greatly relieved.

I also have a tendency to stockpile or gunnysack negative emotions. Often I am so out of touch with what I am feeling that I am not aware of the stockpiling process. Other times I rationalize to myself that these emotions will just go away if I refuse to look at them. Just stack them away and hope they vanish.

An analogy comes to my mind. Last Tuesday I put some left-overs of Caesar salad, grilled fish, avocado and creamed potatoes in the refrigerator. By Saturday the avocado had turned brown, the cream sauce had soured, the salad was wilted, and the fish smelled rotten. If the leftovers had been eaten in twenty-four hours, all would have been well.

Emotions are very similar: deal with them immediately and they can enhance and motivate life. Stuff them away, and they seem to acquire a life of their own. Spoiled food and stuffed emotions must be dealt with; neither will just disappear.

Another observation: when I examined the list of character flaws in Step Seven, I noticed that for me the first five flaws usually manifest themselves in self-talk.

For example, I tend to talk to myself in a pessimistic undertone, pointing out in a disparaging way my lack of perfection and in a vengeful way the shortcomings of the people I resent. I carry on this dialogue often to prevent myself from examining what I am *really* feeling—usually a variation of fear or anger. This self-talk often ambushes me; it's like having a savage bully living inside me.

When all this seems overwhelming, I remind myself that I have gone through Step Three, and God is there to help me minute by minute. I don't have to fight the bully by myself.

QUESTIONS TO ASK MYSELF ABOUT THE TENTH STEP

- Which character flaw causes me the most problems on a daily basis?
- Is there a new problem in my life that I am trying to avoid or deny? Why?
- Do I have a plan for carrying out the Tenth Step?
- Am I noticing improvement in some area of my life?
- If I was in the wrong today in some area, did I promptly admit it?

---

[1] Richard O'Connor, Ph.D., *Undoing Depression: What Therapy Doesn't Teach You and Medication Can't Give You* (New York: Little, Brown and Company, Berkley Books ed., 1999) p. 317.

[2] *Twelve Steps and Twelve Traditions* (New York: Alcoholics Anonymous World Services, Inc. 1994) p. 92.

— Notes —

STEP ELEVEN

> "Sought through prayer and meditation to improve our conscious contact with God *as we understood Him*, praying only for knowledge of His will for us and the power to carry that out."

Having stated that Step Ten is a maintenance step, Step Eleven is maintenance with a plus—prayer and meditation. Basically, prayer is talking to God, and meditation is listening to God.

Step Ten makes us aware of continuing problems; Step Eleven reassures us that the solution is always there.

By Step Ten, we have already experienced many gifts from our Higher Power. He has restored us to sanity; He has removed some of our character defects and shortcomings. In Step Eleven, we determine to know Him better, and prayer and meditation are the pathways to that knowledge.

If you come to Depression Anonymous from a strong religious background, you are already familiar with prayer and meditation. As said before, D.A. does not espouse any theology and instead encourages members to deepen the roots of the faith they already have.

This step is a call to deepen your religious experience. Whatever religious tradition has been in the back of your mind throughout the first ten steps—your Higher Power, the God of your understanding—this step urges you to intensify this experience.

This may mean going back to your church, synagogue, or whatever worship center seems right to you. Get literature about prayer and meditation and use it. There you will find help with prayer and meditation to meet your individual needs.

People speak often of the sense of peace that prayer and meditation brings. Depression makes us feel lonely, lost, purposeless, and frightened; we feel adrift in a hostile world. Prayer and meditation ground us in the realization that we are in the hands of a loving, just God who has a purpose for the world and for us. We can rest in God's hands, knowing we will be strengthened, directed and protected.

Examined closely, one sees that the experience of a clinical depression—the despair, the sense of meaning-lessness in everything, the absence of the ability to feel pleasure, the heaviness in every effort—is the opposite of being in the presence of the creator of the universe.

Twelve-step literature abounds with references to the beneficial power of prayer and meditation:

> In A.A. we have found that the actual good results of prayer are beyond question. They are matters of knowledge and experience. All those who have persisted have found strength not ordinarily their own. They have found wisdom beyond their usual capability. And they have increasingly found a peace of mind which can stand firm in the face of difficult circumstances.[1]

MEMBERS SHARE THEIR
EXPERIENCES WITH THIS STEP

By the time I reached the Eleventh Step, I had become convinced that living life by my own will only led me to chronic depression. I was ready to tread a different path. I felt convinced that if I could stay in touch with God each day and consciously resolve to obey Him, my life would go differently.

I resolved to write down on my daily calendar each day, "Dedicate day to God." I would make a conscious choice to place myself in God's hands for the next twenty-four hours. I would then remind myself of the specific character flaws to look out for today. At present they are the tendency to deny my own real feelings and the inclination to not help another person unless I could see a direct benefit. I would strive to be open all day to the quiet nudgings of the spirit and act upon them.

I further resolved to write down ten things each day for which I was grateful. This would be a daily thanksgiving prayer to God. In my depressions, I had focused on all the things I lacked; this was a small step in the other direction.

Earlier I had joined an Episcopal church close to my home. I had been raised in the Methodist church, but I've also been a member of Presbyterian and Lutheran congregations throughout my life. Even though there are some differences, all of them have nurtured me spiritually.

I tried to build into my day experiences where I would be reconnected with God. I discovered a local Christian radio station and set my car and kitchen radio to that channel. This way I am continually reminded of God and His care for me. My mother had given me about fifteen old copies of *The Upper Room*, an excellent Methodist devotional guide. I put *The Upper Room* close to my toothbrush so that I can focus on a couple of the devotions while my teeth are getting brushed. I admire people who devote an uninterrupted 15 to 30 minutes of time to meditation, but at least there are some connections to God built into my day.

QUESTIONS TO ASK MYSELF ABOUT THE ELEVENTH STEP

- What practical steps can I take today to add prayer and meditation to my life?

- What personal experiences can I call to memory that will strengthen my resolution for a more conscious contact with God?
- Can I honestly pray only for God's will for me?
- Can I truly see how my self-will has caused me difficulty and pain?

— NOTES —

[1]   *Twelve Steps and Twelve Traditions* (New York: Alcoholics Anonymous World Services, Inc. 1994) p. 104.

STEP TWELVE

"Having had a spiritual awakening as the result of these steps, we tried to carry this message to others, and to practice these principles in all our affairs."

Step Twelve is composed of three vital phrases. The first phrase, "Having had a spiritual awakening as the result of these steps," highlights the deeper relationship we now have with the God of our understanding. Some members have had dramatic spiritual experiences; others have had slower, subtler encounters. Nevertheless, there are commonalities that apply to all. The member is now able to say of his spiritual awakening:

> He has been set on a path that tells him he is really going somewhere, that life is not a dead end, not something to be endured or mastered. In a very real sense he has been transformed, because he has laid hold of a source of strength which, in one way or another, he had hitherto denied himself. He finds himself in possession of a degree of honesty, tolerance, unselfishness, peace of mind, and love of which he had thought himself quite incapable.[1]

The second phrase, "we tried to carry this message to others," implicitly states that we share what we've learned in D.A. with other depressives. It means inviting others to meetings, organizing new meetings in parts of the city where there is a need, and supporting meetings with our presence.

There is a larger context of this phrase. Whenever we meet a real human need, we are practicing Step Twelve. One prominent psychiatrist sees the enormous growth of depressed people in the last twenty-five years as a reflection of our society's lack of balance between the needs of self and the needs of others:

> So that is my diagnosis: The epidemic of depression stems from the much-noted rise in individualism and the decline in the commitment to the common good. This means there are two ways out: First, changing the balance of individualism and the commons; second, exploiting the strengths of the maximal self.[2]

What Dr. Seligman proposes as part of the solution to this epidemic of depression is what he calls "moral jogging." He explains that many people in our society have taken up jogging not because they enjoy the exercise, but because they are convinced that jogging is good for them, that their long-range health is at stake.

Moral jogging, doing selfless acts for the good of others, is something he advocates we do for our mental health. "Exercise—not physical but moral—may be the antidepressant tactic we need."[3]

Seligman goes on to suggest various selfless activities: (1) Set aside 5 percent of your income to give away to people in need. (2) Give up some activity which you do regularly for your own pleasure and spend this time instead in an activity devoted to the well-being of others or of the community at large. (3) Pay attention to homeless people and when you determine they are in true need, give them some money. (4) When you read of particularly heroic or despicable acts, write praise or "mend-your-ways" letters. He admonishes depressives to devote time to these endeavors.[4] Seligman believes:

> If you engage in activity in service of the commons long enough, it will gain meaning for you. You may find that you get depressed less easily, that you get sick less often, and that you feel better acting for the common good than indulging in solitary pleasures. Most important, an emptiness

inside you, the meaninglessness that rampant individualism nurtures, will begin to fill.[5]

Other studies echo the same idea; *Self* magazine recently reported:

To live longer, do something nice for someone. A University of Michigan at Ann Arbor study finds that folks who help out, say, by doing a senior's cleaning, are up to 60 percent less apt to die over five years than the uncharitable. Maybe it is better to give than receive.[6]

There are other indications in our society that this spirit is increasing. The slogan appearing in many places, "Commit random acts of kindness and senseless acts of beauty," says it well.

This is the underlying spirit of Step Twelve. We must certainly reach out to other depressives, but it doesn't stop there. The whole spirit of this step is the paradox that we receive healing when we reach out to help another in need. Our religious traditions have been telling us this for centuries.

The last phrase, "to practice these principles in all our affairs" is our biggest challenge. Can we bring the same spirit of love and service into our dealings with family? Often, those closest to us tempt us to resentment and bitterness more than others. Can we practice these principles in our workplace? Can we meet our responsibilities to the world at large? Can we bring a real devotion to the religion of our choice?

MEMBERS SHARE THEIR
EXPERIENCES WITH THIS STEP

I felt that I definitely had a spiritual awakening as a result of the steps. Because I had been going to twelve-step meetings the last eight years, my relationship with God had taken on a new dimension. In two important areas, I noticed definite changes—in ingratitude and perfectionism.

I began to realize how persistently I had focused my heart toward ingratitude. I seldom voiced my thanks to God for the blessings He had given me. My mind seemed to be bent on noticing all the things I *didn't* have. Something would be advertised on TV that I couldn't afford, and I would make a silent gripe to God. One of my friends acquired something that I didn't have, and I immediately thought, "Why not me, God?" I read in the paper about someone winning the lottery, and I felt a surge of anger that I wasn't the winner. This kind of thinking was dwindling.

I worked hard on the perfectionism that had often paralyzed me. I realized that many things could be done as quickly as possible although they were far from perfect. I also learned to distinguish between trying to make something better out of fear and when out of love. When I felt the desire to improve something because I really liked what I was doing and wanted to achieve a certain excellence, I embraced the feeling. This was different from the anxious nervousness I felt when compelled to perfect something out of abject fear.

When I realized that the second phrase, "we tried to carry this message to others," implied not only working with other depressives in Depression Anonymous but in seeking to be of service to anyone in real need, something within me shifted.

Up to that point, I had been careful that any "altruistic" act I performed would somehow benefit me. I did nice things for my family; they would remember and do nice things for me when I needed them. I did favors for my friends; at some point they would probably reciprocate. I had real problems with the kind of anonymous giving that the Bible talks about. I realized that the Twelfth Step was pushing me to that kind of giving; I resolved to give it a try.

"Practicing these principles in all my affairs" is a work in progress.

QUESTIONS TO ASK MYSELF ABOUT
THE TWELFTH STEP

- How would I describe my spiritual awakening?
- What am I doing to carry this message to others?
- Are there times in my life when I'm willing to help someone in need without getting credit for it?
- Do I balk at the idea of service to others?
- Am I practicing these principles in all my affairs?

— NOTES —

[1] *Twelve Steps and Twelve Traditions* (New York: Alcoholics Anonymous World Services, Inc. 1994) p. 107.
[2] Martin E.P. Seligman, Ph.D., *Learned Optimism* (New York: Alfred A. Knopf, 1991) p. 286.
[3] Seligman, p. 288.
[4] Seligman, p. 289.
[5] Seligman, p. 290.
[6] "Score with Chores," *Self*, March 2003, p. 132.

— PART TWO —

PERSONAL STORIES

The personal stories in this section describe the relief from depression achieved by following the principles of the Twelve Steps. Most of the people listed probably did not consciously realize they were following these principles. However, in each case, the healing from depression came about not primarily by medication but by a change in thought and behavior. This is the aim of the Twelve Steps—to bring about a positive change in thought and behavior.

ABRAHAM LINCOLN

Looking back in history, we see examples of people who have experienced depression and nevertheless led productive, useful lives. Looking closely, we see how some of the principles of this program enabled them to triumph in their struggle with depression.

The first historical figure to consider is Abraham Lincoln. Almost everyone has heard of Lincoln's facility with words; many were required in school to memorize "The Gettysburg Address" and other great works of Lincoln. Because of his compassion, sense of fair play, and role in eliminating slavery, he is called "The Great Emancipator." His industry, honesty, and ambition enabled him to rise to the highest office in the nation. Almost everyone has a favorite Abraham Lincoln story.

Few people realize, however, that Abraham Lincoln struggled with depression many times in his life. Historians can give many examples of this. Lincoln's own words testify:

> I am now the most miserable man living. If what I feel were equally distributed to the whole human family, there would not be one cheerful face on earth. Whether I shall ever be better, I cannot tell; I awfully forebode I shall not. To remain as I am is impossible. I must die or be better, it appears to me.[1]

Lincoln appeared to be melancholy so often that his friends were worried about his sanity. At one point, a friend named Bowline Greene carried Lincoln off to his own secluded home and watched him carefully.

Another one of Lincoln's own remarks is telling. He told a fellow legislator that although he seemed to others to enjoy life rapturously, yet when alone he was so overcome by mental depression, he never dared to carry a pocketknife.[2]

Lincoln was also troubled by the kind of depression that seemed to strike "out of the blue"—even on occasions others would consider joyous. Lincoln was so depressed on the day that he was supposed to wed Mary Todd that he did not appear at the ceremony. His friends were alarmed and went searching for him; they found him walking by himself, desperately depressed. Afraid that he might attempt to kill himself, they began a suicide watch over him.[3]

Pictures and statues of Lincoln can verify what his contemporaries noted: "He was a sad-looking man; his melancholy dripped from him as he walked."[4] Still others noted the "melancholy of his face in repose."[5]

Yet, we know that Lincoln triumphed over his bent toward depression; it is an understatement to say he led a productive life. He is universally revered as one of our greatest presidents. In Lincoln's lifetime, there were no psychiatrists, therapists, or anti-depressant medications. Where did Lincoln gain the strength to triumph over depression? The answer can be found primarily in Lincoln's relationship with God.

The spiritual strength that enabled Lincoln to overcome depression was nurtured in his early years. He had very few books to read as a child, but he did have the Bible and *Pilgrim's Progress.* As a child, Lincoln memorized many passages from the Bible as well as many hymns.

Many examples abound where Lincoln refers to God. In a letter to his good friend, Joshua Speed, Lincoln says, "I believe God made me one of the instruments of bringing you and Fanny together."[6] In the speech that Lincoln made before being inaugurated president, he said:

> I now leave . . . with a task before me
> greater than that which rested upon
> Washington. Without the assistance
> of that Divine Being who ever attended

him, I cannot succeed. With that assistance, I cannot fail.[7]

Further evidence of Lincoln's spiritual source of
strength is to be found in another letter he wrote to his
friend, Joshua Speed: "I am profitably engaged in reading the Bible. Take all of this book upon reason that you
can and balance upon faith and you will live and die a
better man."[8] Biographers of Lincoln emphasize that he
loved the Bible and knew it intimately. Lincoln was
captivated by what he called the "true spirit of Christ"
and adopted this as his rule of life.[9]

Another means of fighting depression was writing
poetry; here Lincoln could give vent to his melancholy
feelings. He didn't write great, critically-acclaimed poetry, but writing poetry enabled Lincoln to objectify in
words the feelings inside him.

An additional resource for combating depression
was Lincoln's great sense of humor. He refused to take
himself too seriously. When a political opponent
accused him of being two-faced, Lincoln remarked: "If
I were two-faced, do you think I'd choose to wear *this*
face?"[10]

Lincoln said that, when he heard a preacher, he
liked to see him act as if he were fighting bees.[11] Lincoln
once told a hotel waiter, "If this is coffee, please bring
me some tea; but if this is tea, please bring me some
coffee."[12]

Lincoln had no problem making fun of himself.
Lincoln had served in a local militia during the Black
Hawk War. He later joked that the only blood he had
spilled in defense of his country was mosquito blood.[13]

Another premise of this program "Have an attitude
of gratitude" is seen in the life of Lincoln. Remember
that it was Abraham Lincoln who made Thanksgiving
Day a national holiday by a proclamation he issued in
1863.

In conclusion, even though Lincoln was clearly troubled by the demon of depression in his life, he triumphed. Many of the principles of this program can be seen in the life of Lincoln. He brought God into his life and relied on spiritual guidance in all his affairs. He wrote poetry to get in touch with his feelings. He used the resource of humor to give balance to his life. He fought the tendency toward morose brooding by immersing himself in complex, time-consuming political affairs. He dedicated his life to the service of others.

Lincoln has been often quoted as saying, "Most folks are about as happy as they make up their minds to be"—a statement that is right in line with this program. You *choose* to be happy, to think positive thoughts. You refuse to give in to the negative, self-pitying, unhappy thoughts. Lincoln is an excellent role model for us.

1   Mark S. Gold, MD, *The Good News About Depression* (New York: Villard Books, 1987) p. 190.
2   Lord Charnwood, *Abraham Lincoln* (New York: Madison Books, 1996) p. 63.
3   Gold, p. 190.
4   Ibid.
5   Charnwood, p. 82.
6   Ibid., p. 66.
7   Ibid., p. 150.
8   Ibid., p. 315.
9   Ibid., p. 315.
10 Bob Dole in a television interview talking about his book, *Great Presidential Wit.*
11 Bob Dole, *Great Presidential Wit* (New York: Simon & Schuster, 2001) p. 29.
12 Ibid., p. 34.
13 Ibid., p. 29.

WINSTON CHURCHILL

Another historical figure known to have battled depression is Winston Churchill. Definitely one of the most important figures in English history, he is famous for rallying his fellow citizens to resist Hitler. "He was a lion of a man who helped shape the course of this century with his relentless ambition and fierce political instincts."[1]

Churchill's battle with depression began early in his life. When he was a young schoolboy at Harrow, the first recorded instance of his depression came. At that time, he seemed sunk in misery and gloom with the "near-suicidal affliction which...would plague him at intervals throughout his life."[2]

Then, as a young man he became a soldier in the Cuban War; the regimental life plunged him again into misery and gloom. One historian writes:

> To understand this stage in Churchill's life, one must understand the power of depression and the agony endured by the true depressive. This is in a class removed from the normal person's feelings of unhappiness or of "feeling down." It brings the constant pain of utter hopelessness. It causes total isolation and despair. . . .This was the situation, which, at twenty-one, Churchill realized he had to cope.[3]

In searching for the cause of Churchill's depressions (which he called the "Black Dog"), genetic factors must be considered; depression ran in the Churchill family. His brother, John, is described as having a markedly depressive temperament. In addition, historians report that at least five of Churchill's ancestors suffered from melancholia.[4]

Churchill's depression was sometimes so intense that he was suicidal. He stated that at railway stations he avoided the edge of the platform when a train was passing. He also avoided the sides of ships and would not look down at the water. "'A second's action would end everything. A few drops of desperation . . . .' he told Charles Moran, his doctor. The only thing that seemed to help, he said, was to 'talk it over with Clementine.'"[5]

Besides talking things over with his wife, Clementine, Churchill had another way to fight his depression—aggression. His aggressive temperament had brought him success throughout his military career. It had helped him overcome some cowardly fears and brought him much success in politics. Aggression could transform him into a hero unconcerned about danger.[6]

One example of Churchill's aggressive, determined stance in fighting depression can be seen by examining one of his legendary speeches. In 1941, Prime Minister Churchill was asked to speak to the boys at Harrow, the school he had attended earlier. He stood up before the students.

"Never give up. Never, never, never give up. Never give up!"

Then he sat down.

It is astounding that a man plagued by depression, an illness that has prompted many throughout history to give up, should voice such inspiring words. Perhaps Churchill was talking as much to himself as to his listeners.

Churchill found another way to deal with his depressions; he took up painting as a hobby. He even wrote a book about it, *Painting as a Pastime*. He was able to sublimate his aggression and curb his anxieties by painting. It also diverted his mind from chronic worry, "a spasm of the emotion; the mind catches hold of something and will not let it go."[7]

Churchill wrote numerous other books, so it is clear that he found release in writing; he thought composition to be true happiness. "He wrote long books about complex matters, constantly moving between the battlefield and the inner circles of government."[8] With a busy schedule like Churchill's, little time was left for obsessive thoughts.

Another release was in humor. Churchill was known for his wit. When Nancy Astor said to him: "If I were your wife I would put poison in your coffee!" Churchill replied, "And if I were your husband, I would drink it."[9] Churchill once remarked on the comic relationship between living things: "Dogs look up to us. Cats look down on us. Pigs treat us as equals."[10]

Before the first night of *Pygmalion*, George Bernard Shaw wired Churchill: "Am reserving two tickets for you for my premiere. Come and bring a friend—if you have one." Churchill replied: "Impossible to be present for the first performance. Will attend the second—if there is one."[11]

On the occasion of his seventy-fifth birthday, Churchill said, "I am prepared to meet my Maker. Whether my Maker is prepared for the great ordeal of meeting me is another matter."[12]

The mind that is constantly focusing on witty, humorous things to say has less time for resentful rumination. Churchill's coping mechanisms exemplify principles of the Depression Anonymous program. "Do play—find recreation and hobbies" and "Don't get stuck in obsessive thoughts" are part of the slogans read at each meeting.

Perhaps the strongest element of the Depression Anonymous program exemplified in Churchill was the great release he found in talking about his depressions to his wife, Clementine. He stated that at times this was the *only* thing that helped him. This program is built on sharing; when we can talk about how we feel with others, we find comfort and strength.

[1]   John Pearson, *The Private Lives of Winston Churchill* (New York:
      Simon & Schuster, 1991) book cover commentary.
[2]   Ibid., p. 78.
[3]   Ibid., p. 80.
[4]   Ibid., p. 28.
[5]   Ibid., p. 129.
[6]   Ibid., p. 131.
[7]   Ibid., p. 158.
[8]   Norman Rose, *Churchill: The Unruly Giant* (New York: The Free
      Press, 1994) p. 258.
[9]   Ibid., p. 250.
[10] Ibid., p. 251.
[11] Gretchen Rubin, *Forty Ways to Look at Winston Churchill* (New
      York: Ballantine Books, 2003) p. 56.
[12] Geoffrey Best, *Churchill: A Study in Greatness* (New York: Oxford
      University Press, 2003) p. 329.

Bill Wilson

Another historical character that dealt with severe depression was the co-founder of Alcoholics Anonymous, Bill Wilson.

Psychologists state that depression tends to run in families. Certainly this was evident in the life of Winston Churchill and here also in Bill Wilson's life. Bill suspected that depression ran in his mother's family; he remembered as a child that his mother had frequent "nervous breakdowns." He recalled that she was once away in a sanitarium.[1]

Psychologists also tell us that early personal losses seem to precipitate depression. When Bill was about nine years old, his parents divorced. This was a shock that Bill never forgot. He was separated from the father he adored and didn't see him for nine years. "Bill said he remained depressed for almost a year following his parents' divorce."[2]

Another personal loss occurred when Bill was seventeen. He had fallen deeply in love with Bertha Bamford, daughter of the town's Episcopal minister. Bertha, a beautiful, popular girl, returned Bill's love; Bertha's parents liked Bill and welcomed him in their home.[3]

Then came the news that Bertha had died suddenly. She had an operation for the removal of a tumor at Flower Hospital in New York City. The operation seemed successful, but Bertha died during the night from an internal hemorrhage.

For Bill, it meant total anguish. "It eventuated in what was called an old-fashioned nervous breakdown, which meant, I now realize, a tremendous depression."[4] This marked the beginning of a three-year depression. "Interest in everything except the fiddle collapsed. No athletics, no schoolwork done, no attention to anyone. I was utterly, deeply, and compulsively miserable, convinced that my whole life had utterly collapsed."[5]

Meeting Lois Burnham (who would become his wife) finally lifted Bill out of his deep depression. On their wedding day, Bill's depressive turn of mind surfaced; he was conscious of horrible feelings of inferiority. He imagined that some of Lois's family and friends were snidely remarking, "Where did Lois get that one?"[6] This was all in his mind, however, for he was enthusiastically welcomed into Lois's family.

Most people are familiar by now with the great struggle that Bill had with alcoholism. "Terror, self-hatred, and suicidal thoughts became his constant companions. . . . Death seemed to him the only escape from his agony; again and yet again, he contemplated suicide—by poison, by jumping out the window. Accounts differ as to whether it was he or Lois who dragged the mattress downstairs so that he could sleep where an upstairs window would not tempt him to jump."[7]

The turning point in Bill's deliverance from alcoholism came with an astounding spiritual experience. He had reached the lowest point in his life. In desperation Bill cried out to God, "I'll do anything, anything at all! If there be a God, let Him show Himself!"[8]

What happened next was an experience so amazing that Bill would never again doubt the existence of God. "Suddenly, my room blazed with an indescribably white light. I was seized with an ecstasy beyond description. Every joy I had known was pale by comparison. The light, the ecstasy—I was conscious of nothing else for a time."[9] Bill never took another drink after this.

Bill and Dr. Bob Smith set about the task of organizing A.A. groups all over the country. This was a busy, productive time. For ten years, Bill was free of depression. Then in 1944, Bill was "plunged into a depression so black that its effect on him was more debilitating than a physical assault."[10] The depression was totally unexpected because it came after his profound spiritual

experience and the great joy of seeing his vision of A.A.
become a reality.

"There are many and varied accounts of Bill's recur-
rent depression, and almost as many opinions about its
nature, its causes, its intensity, its dynamics and its
manifestations."[11] Aside from the pain of the depression
itself, it was humiliating for Bill to acknowledge that he
was frequently depressed.

Bill investigated many avenues to gain relief from
his depressions. One activity that greatly helped was
walking each day. Thyroid pills helped somewhat. Bill
himself analyzed the problem of his depression this
way:

> Part of the answer lies in a constant effort to
> practice all of the A.A. Twelve Steps. Persistence
> will cause this (depression) to sink in and affect
> that unconscious from where the trouble stems. I
> used to be ashamed of my condition and didn't
> talk about it. But in recent years, I freely confess
> I'm a depressive, and that attracts other depressives
> to me. Working on them has helped a great deal. In
> fact, it helped me more than it did them."[12]

It's noteworthy that Bill didn't just lie around and
give in to the inertia of his depressions. The years of his
depressions (1944-1955) were also the years when he
did the "most exhausting and intensive work for A.A."[13]
All his work during this period was done in spite his
depressions: "sometimes so heavy and black that it took
a heroic effort to get out of bed in the morning."[14]

The happy ending to this story is that from 1955 to
his death in 1971, Bill was free of depression. His feeling
was that if he conscientiously worked the steps long
enough, his depression problems would be over. No
one has come up with a more plausible explanation for
the abrupt cessation of his depression. His story brings
hope and inspiration to many sufferers.

[1] *'Pass It On'* (New York: Alcoholics Anonymous World Services, Inc., 2002) p. 24.
[2] *Pass*, p. 25.
[3] *Pass*, p. 35.
[4] *Pass*, p. 35.
[5] *Pass*, p. 36.
[6] *Pass*, p. 58.
[7] *Pass*, p. 106.
[8] *Pass*, p. 120-121.
[9] *Pass*, p. 121.
[10] *Pass*, p. 292.
[11] *Pass*, p. 292-293.
[12] *Pass*, p. 299.
[13] *Pass*, p. 303.
[14] *Pass*, p. 303.

TRACY THOMPSON

A personal story that illustrates how the principles of this program promote recovery from depression is that of Tracy Thompson. Tracy is a well-regarded reporter for the *Washington Post* and a finalist for a Pulitzer Prize in investigative reporting. Her book, *The Beast: A Reckoning with Depression*, records her lifelong battle with this disease. So many of her feelings in the grip of a depression are familiar.

Tracy writes that she can't enjoy anything:

> There is a deep, gnawing sadness at the core of everything, everything, and on afternoons like this I feel it most. I am empty inside. There is something in the future which is coming. . . I am afraid that it will suck out my core and I will be completely empty and anguished.[1]

Tracy goes on to describe thoughts of suicide, hospitalization for depression, and numerous struggles with the disease. "I feel angry in a dozen ways, all bursting out at once, yet all directed inward."[2] She speaks of her inability to concentrate and an unreasonable sense of panic.

Many who are depression-prone can identify with Tracy. The powerlessness to escape from this "thing" and the ensuing panic are experiences others have related in meetings.

The good news is that, while Tracy sometimes had thoughts of suicide, she didn't end up as a suicide statistic. She slowly recovers from her depression. She begins to realize that her mental attitudes have a profound effect on the course of her depression, and she consciously starts to change some of her thought and behavior patterns.

Tracy writes of creating a program of recovery for herself:

I was struck by the similarities between the *ad hoc* program I created for myself that summer and the twelve-step recovery method of Alcoholics Anonymous and Narcotics Anonymous. Their goals tracked closely with mine: honesty in all things, especially with myself; clear understanding of my strengths and weaknesses; the laying aside of defensiveness and pride to accept help from others; the sometimes painful moving away from people who could not support my efforts.[3]

Tracy elaborates on her first goal "honesty in all things." "At some point, honesty—excruciating, self-lacerating, merciless honesty—becomes the only antidote, the only agent strong enough to tear through the mental labyrinth created by all those walls of denial."[4]

Honesty is an essential part of all twelve-step programs. The Big Book of A.A. speaks of people who fail in their recovery efforts because they are "constitutionally incapable of being honest with themselves. . . . They are naturally incapable of grasping and developing a manner of living which demands rigorous honesty."[5]

In another section of the Big Book, the alcoholic prior to recovery is characterized as a dishonest person who "leads a double life. He is very much the actor. To the outer world he presents his stage character." If he is to recover, the alcoholic must see himself as he really is and share that vision with another human being. To find healing, the alcoholic must be "entirely honest with somebody."[6]

Tracy speaks about another important element in her recuperation—learning the difference between feeling shame and taking responsibility. She finds that shame is to be avoided; it is "a way to wallow in . . . feelings without doing anything about them."[7]

This emphasis on taking responsibility for one's own mental health is a constant theme in recovery literature. "So our troubles, we think, are basically of our own making,"[8] the Big Book of A.A. states. "In my experience, the most crucial predictor of recovery is a persistent willingness to exert some effort to help yourself,"[9] says Dr. David Burns, a renowned psychiatrist.

Tracy also emphasizes the necessity of not indulging in self-pity. She found a button with the word "WHINE" printed with a slash through it. At the bottom was printed, "NO WHINING ALLOWED." She put the button permanently on her bulletin board as a silent reminder of what she calls "tough self-love." She learned to love herself and forgive her mistakes but was tough on herself if tempted to whine and complain.

Tracy's book ends on an optimistic note. There is no doubt in her mind that her recovery from depression has been accelerated in the past four years. Now there is a peace, joy, and confidence in her life that was not there previously. She believes that she was born with a predisposition to suffer from depression, which developed into clinical depression as a result of stressful life events. She believes that emotions are partly learned and "can be relearned—with help."[10]

Her book closes with a list of what she calls, "The Rules":

Honesty in all things, large and small (social and job exceptions as required).

When you are angry, express it, resolve it if possible, then forget it. No grudges.

Admit mistakes promptly and make amends if possible.

Help others. Be of service. Only in this way will you find your way out of the prison of self...[11]

The first rule about honesty has already been discussed. The second rule, "When you are angry .... No grudges" is echoed in the Big Book of A.A.: "Resentment is the 'number one' offender. It destroys more alcoholics than anything else. .... It is plain that a life, which includes deep resentment, leads only to futility and unhappiness."

The alcoholic is cautioned that his very life depends on his being free of anger. He simply cannot afford to be a grouch.[12]

The third rule phrase, "Admit mistakes promptly," is very similar to the Tenth Step phrase, "when we were wrong promptly admitted it." The last part of the third rule, "make amends if possible" sounds so much like the Ninth Step, "Made direct amends to such people whenever possible." The fourth rule has essentially the same ideas as the Twelfth Step.

Tracy's life is now full of strength and hope. She has demonstrated that changing her thoughts and behavior changes depression. By being proactive in her own recovery, Tracy is an inspiration to others suffering from depression. She is committed to continuing the process that she has so successfully begun.

---

[1]   *The Beast: A Reckoning with Depression* by Tracy Thompson, copyright © 1995 by Tracy Thompson. Used by permission of G. P. Putnam's Sons, a division of Penguin Group (USA) Inc., New York, p. 47.

[2]   Ibid, p. 46.

[3]   Ibid, p. 235.

[4]   Ibid, p. 236.

[5]   *Alcoholics Anonymous* (New York: Alcoholics Anonymous World Services, Inc., 2001) p. 58.

[6]   Ibid, pp. 73-74.

[7]   Thompson, p. 236.

[8]   *Alcoholics Anonymous*, p. 62.

[9]   David D. Burns, M.D., *Feeling Good: The New Mood Therapy* (New York: William Morrow and Co., Inc., 1980) p. 16.

[10] Thompson, p. 285.

[11] Ibid, p. 286.

[12] *Alcoholics Anonymous*, pp. 64-66.

RICHARD O'CONNOR, PH.D.

Dr. Richard O'Connor is another person who experienced depression and overcame it. Currently director of the Northwest Center for Family Service and Mental Health in Connecticut, he is a psychotherapist and author of the book *Undoing Depression: What Therapy Doesn't Teach You and Medication Can't Give You.*

When Richard was fifteen, a devastating experience turned his world upside down. He came home from school one day to find that his mother had committed suicide in the basement. She had bolted the doors and taped a note to the window saying she was out shopping and he should wait at a neighbor's house. Knowing something was wrong, he was climbing in a window when his father came driving in after work. They discovered her body together.[1]

This marked the beginning of Richard's struggle with depression—although he didn't call it that at the time. He just knew he felt unhappy, angry at the world, suspicious, and reserved. He wanted very much to be loved but was "afraid to trust—a sure setup for depression."[2]

Richard found high school easy and reveled in being the academic star. Problems developed, however, when he went to college and competed with others just as bright as he was. He became scared, depressed, and desperate to fit in. He started mixing alcohol and pills, the same sleeping pills his mother had used. There were nights when he didn't care if he woke up in the morning.[3]

Something motivated him to get help. He went to various therapists over the years in an effort to put a label on his problems. Along the way, he became a psychotherapist and earned a Ph.D. There were long periods in his life when he drank too much, when he alienated everyone close to him, when he could just barely get to work, when he would wake up each morning hating the thought of facing his life. Life seemed so miserable, hopeless, and joyless that he wished for a way out. Many times he thought of suicide.

Though he still struggles with the emotional habits of depression, he believes those days are behind him. His life now has purpose and joy. In his recovery journey, he has learned many things that benefit other depressives.[4]

Richard O'Connor wrote the book *Undoing Depression* to record what he has learned in his recovery from depression and assist other depressives in unlearning the habits of depression. He believes that many people have experienced depression for so long that they feel it is what they *are*. But he insists that depression is something you *have*—just like you might have heart disease.

Dr. O'Connor believes that without realizing it, depressives get good at depression. They learn how to hide it and how to work around it. They are skilled at hiding their feelings from themselves, at stuffing their feelings and skilled in negative thinking. These "skills" become habits; however, these habits can be unlearned so that the depressive can find true recovery, deep joy and healthy emotions.

It is interesting to note that Dr. O'Connor's advice to depressives in undoing the habits of depression is to be a member of a group similar to Depression Anonymous:

> We've found that the experience of dealing with depression in a self-help context is very positive. We've also found that the model and structure of AA are very useful for depression. Depression is a disease the way alcoholism is a disease—recovery comes only from a change in behavior.[5]

Dr. O'Connor mentions many times in his book the value of support groups in assisting recovery:

It will be easier if you can join a support group. Try to find one in your local community. Ask the local mental health center and the local hospital if they sponsor such groups.... But if you can't find a group you like, don't be afraid to start one.... It's the group experience, the process of discussing and digesting ideas like these, that cures. The sharing, support, and confrontation provide us with a safe place to practice the skills we need to undo our depression.[6]

In a lighter vein, Dr. O'Connor speaks of how playing with his children was therapeutic for him. He would come home each night and play silly games with them. He'd drag them around the polished floor on sheets, play train, or hide under an old mattress. His own childhood was cold and scary; his children helped him make up for some of what he had missed.

Dr. O'Connor recently celebrated his forty-eighth birthday. For years he had believed that he wouldn't live past his thirty-eighth. (This was his mother's age when she took her life.) He was long obsessed with the idea that he couldn't outlive her, that whatever drove her over the edge would catch up with him.[7]

Dr. O'Connor has come to terms with his depression; in the process of undoing the habits of depression himself, he has given hope and inspiration to many.

---

[1]   Richard O'Connor, Ph.D., *Undoing Depression: What Therapy Doesn't Teach You and Medication Can't Give You* (New York: Little, Brown and Company; Berkley Books ed., 1999) pp. 6-7.

[2]   O'Connor, p. 62.

[3]   O'Connor, p. 302.

[4]   O'Connor, pp. 7-8.

[5]   O'Connor, pp. 204-205.

[6]   O'Connor, p. 318.

[7]   O'Connor, p. 301. He stated here that this is a common belief with children of suicides; Ted Turner, for instance, had this belief.

JEFFERY SMITH

Another contemporary who experienced depression is Jeffery Smith, author of *Where the Roots Reach for Water: A Personal & Natural History of Melancholia*. Jeffery brilliantly describes the negative self-talk, the internal voice of condemnation, familiar to depressives:

> I had given him—that voice, I mean—a name: Mr. Shoulder, I called him, because when I first made his acquaintance it seemed he was perched on my shoulder, watching and whispering into my ear.... By now he was with me loud and clear, shrill of voice, sharp of tongue, and painfully all-seeing. He would tell me who I was, and his judgment was lacerating, merciless. On the face of it he seemed to be no friend. But there was this: he knew my past, every moment of it and in particular detail, as no stranger could, and nothing was too trivial to escape his notice. He gathered all this intimate data into the great sweeping arguments he used to forecast my future: at every enterprise I would fail. . . Over and over again he told me: You are haunted. You are hollow. You are beyond forgiveness and beyond hope. There is no point vowing to change.[1]

Jeffery recounts many bouts with depression. On one occasion, his girlfriend, Barbara, had just broken up with him mainly because she couldn't tolerate his persistent low moods. He was feeling that life had lost all of its savor; all pleasure in experience and thought had vanished.[2] In addition, he experienced a leaden lethargy and fatigue:

> It seemed all I could do just to get myself to the office in the morning.... At the office every phone call, every home visit, every bit of documentation felt like drudgery. I was a month behind on my

paperwork. At home I'd toss my mail, the bills along with the letters, into the corner, unopened. I hadn't balanced my own checkbook for a month. A pile of overdue library books sat on my kitchen table. I drove past the public library at least once a day, but it seemed more than I could manage to call to mind the necessary foresight, and lift the books off the table, and then carry them to my car, and then drop them off at the library. Any one of those steps was a challenge; accomplishing them consecutively was well-nigh impossible.[3]

Jeffery's problems with sleep also mirror the experience of many depressives:

> I was awake every morning at four, after finally falling asleep just a couple hours before. I was unable to return to sleep, but neither could I will myself out of bed. I couldn't summon the concentration to read, so I would lie abed for three more hours, staring at the ceiling until it was time to go to work. I was exhausted; but I could not get the sleep to remedy it. When it was time to ready myself for work the stairway to the kitchen and bathroom seemed too steep to climb, and then my arms felt too heavy to lift and wash myself in the shower. So I just stood in there under the water.[4]

He couldn't see his way out of the depression; he felt desperate. Earlier he had tried the antidepressant, Zoloft, and it had worked for about two months. Then, abruptly, he was right back where he had started with his depression.

He tried many other antidepressant medications — alone and in combination. All met with the same result; they would work fine for a short while, and then he was back at ground zero. His doctor told him that he had treatment-resistant depression.

Depression became a malevolent presence that he could not reason away. It was impervious to all his plans and wishes and was not affected by external events. Depression had taken over his life, and Jeffery had reached the point where death was preferable.

He considered many forms of suicide— overdosing on pills, drowning, shooting a gun, and carbon monoxide poisoning. For Jeffery the future appeared as only an endless succession of the present pain. "Just drawing breath after odious, laborious, stale breath begins to seem pointless,"[5] he states at that point.

His turning point came when he began taking a new antidepressant in addition to the other two he had been taking. He became paralyzed and was taken to the emergency room; no one could give an adequate explanation for the paralysis, but he became convinced that it was caused by the combined effects of the three antidepressants. Since the pills were not really helping him, he decided to dispense with pills altogether. "I didn't know, but something within me shifted that day. . . ."[6]

Up to that point, Jeffery had been a lifelong cynic. He began to open some doors to faith in God. He studied some Appalachian folk hymns and discovered the old hymn, "Wayfaring Stranger." The words captivated him, especially the second stanza:

> I know dark clouds will hover o'er me.
> I know my pathway's rough and steep.
> But beauteous fields lie out before me
> Where God's redeem'd their vigils keep.

He also started to read extensively about depression; he began with the ancients who termed it "melancholia". The more he learned about the disease, the more optimistic he became.

His therapist photocopied a chapter from Evelyn Underhill's *Mysticism*[7] entitled "The Dark Night of the

Soul." The chapter described the experiences of various saints—John of the Cross, Meister Eckhart, Teresa of Avila and many others. Jeffery observed that while Underhill used the word depression only once, the experiences of these saintly people reflected the state of depression.

The book *Mysticism* goes on to suggest that while in the grips of this "dark night of the soul" the presence of God seems to have vanished, the dark night became for these saints a growth stage to a deeper relationship with God. This idea filled Jeffery with great hope.

Jeffery later consulted a friend of his, a Methodist minister. He said to his friend: "I am nobody's victim. All my messes are my own doing. There is nobody I need to forgive but myself. So how do I do that?"[8]

His minister friend responded by telling Jeffery that his big problem was that he refused to accept the forgiveness of God:

> "I am worthless," you keep saying. "I can't do anything," you keep saying. It's just as bad as pride, I'd say, your obsession with your sins and shortcomings: just as self-important. . . . You worship a graven idol, and that idol is your self. You need to get out of your own way. Forgiveness—for you, forgiving yourself—will relieve you of that burden. . . . Here's my advice, old friend: put your self in the hands of something bigger and wiser than you.[9]

Jeffery then describes how he took his friend's advice; the positive effect was amazing. Jeffery states that he still considers depression a kind of "walking death", but "now I accounted the death part of it differently. This death was a yielding; I would, like any pilgrim, surrender my affairs into the hands of God."[10]

Jeffery relates how his life began to improve. He became close to his family again. He fell in love and was married. He found satisfying work.

Jeffery's book closes with a chapter that is essentially a gratitude list. He especially thanks all the people who assisted him in his life journey. He closes the book with: "And my thanks to our Almighty Creator. For everything, even melancholia."[11]

[1]   *Where the Roots Reach for Water: A Personal & Natural History of Melancholia* by Jeffery Smith. Copyright © 1999 by Jeffery Smith. Reprinted by permission of North Point Press, a division of Farrar, Straus and Giroux, LLC. p. 11.

[2]   Smith, p. 18.

[3]   Smith, p. 10.

[4]   Smith, p. 7.

[5]   Smith, p. 21.

[6]   Smith, p. 24.

[7]   Evelyn Underhill, *Mysticism: The Nature and Development of Spiritual Consciousness* (New York: Doubleday, 1990). (This book was originally published in 1911.)

[8]   Smith, p. 199.

[9]   Smith, p. 199.

[10] Smith, p. 223.

[11] Smith, p. 280.

Susan's Story

Another person who has battled depression is a lady named Susan. Losses in life often predispose a person to depression; Susan had two painful losses prior to the onset of her depression. A psychotherapist who has worked extensively with depressed patients comments, "Death of a parent at an early age or loss of the parental relationship...certainly seems to make people susceptible [to depression]."[1]

Susan's beloved mother was only in her early forties when she died of breast cancer. About the same time, Susan lost a baby boy after a six and a half months' pregnancy. She sank into a pit of depression.

This all occurred in the 1960s when depression was not as common as it is today. Furthermore, Susan was a minister's wife who felt that is was not Christian to be depressed. So, she hid her depression from the congregation.

She consulted various psychiatrists. One told her that her depression was caused because she felt guilty over her miscarriage. Another gave her strong medication that had an adverse effect on her body. The depression became much worse. She stated that she was encouraged to get very angry and blame others for what caused any measure of turmoil.

The depression led to attempts at suicide; after one attempt she was in a coma for three days. The abyss of depression lasted for five years. Since five years of psychiatric treatment had not yielded any peace, she decided on a whole new approach. She discontinued all medications for depression.

During this time she read a book (which she does not name) that essentially said, "You're not irresponsible because you're sick; you're sick because you're irresponsible." In other words, you need to take full responsibility for your thoughts and for your actions. Don't blame anyone else.

She began to think constantly about being responsible for every thought and for every action. Acting responsibly became the stair steps for her climb out of the pit of depression.

She gained an important insight on her problem from one of her husband's sermons on forgiveness. His text was Matthew 18:21-35—the parable of the unforgiving servant. The parable explains that the king was so angry with the unforgiving servant that he sent him to jail to be tortured. "So my heavenly Father will also do to every one of you, if you do not forgive your brother or sister from your heart."[2]

Susan felt herself to be in a state of torture. She began to examine all her relationships carefully to detect where she had been unforgiving. In the process, she came to realize that she had unrealistic expectations and thus blamed other for things she thought they should have done. She realized that she had not accepted responsibility for her own actions.

To further pinpoint her unforgiving spirit, her Bible study leader encouraged Susan to take out a stack of paper and record a different name on each sheet—a name of a person with whom she had conflict. Susan was told to record what he/she had done to her that brought pain and everything she had ever done to hurt them.

Her Bible study leader then encouraged her to look at her lists from Jesus' perspective. Susan found this changed her thinking regarding the entire dynamic of every relationship. The next step was to go to each person and ask their forgiveness—-with no blame whatsoever for anything they had done. It was only for the purpose of asking them to forgive her.

She decided to approach those with the longest list of grievances first, so she started with her father. Her father had almost killed her mother one evening by choking her. He had asked her mother for a divorce when her mom was dying of cancer. He had a terrible temper, and he had beaten Susan when she was growing up.

But none of these things were mentioned when she went to talk with her father. She had forgiven her father for these things when she examined her lists from Jesus' perspective. This was not about her dad: this was about her—what *she* had done that was not right in their relationship.

She acknowledged many positive things about her dad: he had been a wonderful provider; he had given her common sense in the midst of hardship; he was diligent and a very hard worker. She told him that she honored these qualities and that she loved him. Her father's response was wonderful, and she embraced him.

The next on her list was her mother-in-law, Mary. The two women had never gotten along very well—a not uncommon experience. Susan and her husband had been married for fifteen years by this time, and the relationship between the two women remained icy.

Mary had told them not to bring the grandchildren over to her home because she was afraid they would break her precious glass and china items. Susan was offended by this and blamed her mother-in-law for not wanting to have a relationship with their children. Every encounter between the two women was uncomfortable.

When the time was right, Susan told Mary how sorry she was for not having loved her as she should have, for not having honored her as her husband's mother, and for taking issue with her about so many things. She asked her mother-in-law to forgive her. Astounded, Mary readily forgave Susan, and their relationship began on a new basis.

Susan states that she has not suffered from depression since that time. Susan feels that she has been freed from unrealistic expectations, freed from blaming, freed from creating caricatures of people. She believes the entire process of writing names on pieces of paper and asking forgiveness was healing. She truly forgave these people from her heart, and her depression was lifted.

We can immediately see the resemblances between Susan's experience and the twelve-step experience. The process of writing the names of people with whom she had a conflict relates to the Fourth, Eighth and Ninth Steps.

The emphasis on getting rid of unrealistic expectations, being responsible, ceasing to blame others, and paying attention to our own part in problems are themes repeatedly stressed in A.A. and Al-Anon literature.

Susan's healing from depression sends an important message and is an inspiration to all.

[1]   Richard O'Connor, Ph.D., *Undoing Depression: What Therapy Doesn't Teach You and Medication Can't Give You* (New York: Little, Brown and Co., Berkley Books ed., 1999) p. 61.
[2]   *The Holy Bible*, New Revised Standard Version (Michigan: Zondervan Publishing, 1989).

KATHY'S STORY

Another contemporary story of hope — relief from depression following the principles of the twelve-steps —is found in the experience of a girl named Kathy.[1]

Kathy came from a stress-filled family of twelve. Depression, manic-depression, and alcoholism ran in her family for several generations. Both of her parents suffered from untreated depression.

Kathy became the caretaker child, the family hero — getting good grades, babysitting, and doing the housework in a chaotic household. One brother attempted suicide by overdosing on pills. Another brother became ill at fifteen with manic-depression. Two other brothers were involved with drugs. Kathy tried to be the stabilizing force in the family.

She left home and started drinking when she was eighteen years old. Drinking made her forget the depression that had already started taking over her life. Drinking made her feel less lonely, sleep better, feel less anxious and guilty.

Kathy was in denial about her depression. She told herself that she was just weak and disorganized. She never felt up and energetic. To get through each day, she would call her sisters long distance. In one conversation, she asked her sister, Mary, "Don't you feel like I do?" She thought everyone felt life was simply to be endured.

Mary said, "No. I don't. Everyone gets down once in a while, but you're always down. It's not normal. Something is wrong with you."[2]

This started Kathy thinking about getting some help. She had been taking a human relations course to maintain her teaching license, and the kindly instructor, Mildred, took a real interest in her. Mildred said to Kathy, "You're not telling anyone how badly you really feel, are you?" Mildred asked Kathy if she was thinking of hurting herself.

Kathy began to sob and said in a weak voice, "I can't stand this anymore. I just can't stand it anymore."[3]

Mildred offered to help her get into a good hospital nearby. Reluctantly, Kathy agreed. At this point, Kathy couldn't seem to stop crying. She couldn't believe that all this was happening. She had spent her whole life trying to be good, and now everything in her life seemed to be falling apart. She felt like the ultimate failure. Here she was, checking into a psychiatric unit of a hospital.

Kathy says, "I was moving in slow motion. I couldn't stop sighing. Whoever I thought I was, was receding down a dark narrow tunnel; nothing seemed to matter anymore."[4]

Kathy stayed in the hospital one month, with another month of outpatient treatment. The hospital provided therapy, learning and healing. Kathy asked the experts about her case and was not happy with their diagnosis. They said that she had a dual disorder: she was depressed and addicted to alcohol.

Eventually, she accepted the diagnosis and began to deal with her problems. She decided to be an active participant in her own recovery. She felt that she was being asked to change everything in her life without an idea of how it would all turn out. However, she chose to believe that the changes would bring improvement.

Eventually, she was able to say:

I saw and felt myself getting better. . . . I was finding hope again after more than ten years of feeling none. I made friends with some of the patients, dear friends I still have. I learned that I could reach out for help and someone would be there. I was born into a new existence. If, as they say, happiness is directly proportional to how grateful one is, I am happy. I have gained a faith in myself I never had.[5]

Kathy mentions that at times she feels tempted to drink or surrender to hopelessness. She comments on these temptations:

> Fortunately, I now see them as thoughts racing past — like a fast-scrolling message across a computer screen. I can read them, but I don't have to act on them. I have choices. . . . I can't prevent the thoughts from arising in my brain, but I don't have to let them command my behavior. I can watch them flicker across the screen in my head.[6]

Kathy closes by stating that going to AA meetings each week helps her recovery from alcoholism and depression. The meetings counteract the isolation that afflicted her so much of her life; she has developed a deep bond with the people in her A.A. group. She keeps a journal and writes poetry. She has started graduate school and is looking into a career change. "Day by day, I am finding contentment in my life,"[7] she is at last able to say.

[1]   From *The Dual Disorders Recovery Book*, copyright © 1993 by Hazelden Foundation. Reprinted by permission of Hazelden Foundation, Center City, Minnesota, pp. 190-198.
[2]   Hazelden, p. 194.
[3]   Hazelden, p. 195.
[4]   Hazelden, p. 196.
[5]   Hazelden, p. 197.
[6]   Hazelden, p. 198.
[7]   Hazelden, p. 198.

MARILYN'S STORY

When the depression hit me following the birth of my son in 1956, I didn't have a name for it. People didn't talk about depression in those days; I had never heard of postpartum depression. At first I didn't feel the overwhelming sadness and futility, just a pervasive fatigue. I wanted to stay in bed all the time; it was an effort just to lift my arm. I thought something must be terribly wrong with me, so I immediately went to our family doctor. He gave me a clean bill of health. Perplexed, I endeavored to function despite my feelings.

About twenty years later, I realized that I had been predisposed for adult depression by an incest experience with my uncle when I was five years old. (Children who are physically or sexually abused are statistically more prone to adult depression.) For about six months, my parents would have my nineteen-year-old uncle baby-sit for me. What he had me do to him is defined in *Webster's Dictionary* as "fellatio". I only knew then that it was something I didn't like and something I was warned "never to tell anyone about or I would be in real trouble". In 1956 I had never told anyone about this experience and had almost forgotten it entirely.

In 1956, besides the new baby boy, I had a one-year-old girl who was beginning to walk and get into things. My husband was a Presbyterian minister who had recently suffered a severe nervous breakdown; he had been in a mental hospital for five months. I was very eager to preserve his mental health and considered myself to be the strong one emotionally.

My husband had a huge problem with anger; today I call him a "rageaholic." From my perspective, he had a temper flare-up about every other day. I was the logical person to receive his anger. Vent it on church members, and he would soon be out of a job. I felt that I was strong enough to absorb his anger and still maintain my emotional balance. That proved to be dead wrong.

I ended up taking his anger personally. I internalized the feeling that if I were a better wife, he would not be so constantly angry. Today, I can see the foolishness of this approach, but this is the idea that motivated me at the time. When nothing that I did ended the temper tantrums, I started storing up resentment against him; my feelings about him were characterized by resentment and fear.

The constant resentment and fear began to chip away at the real love I originally had for him. The resentment and fear were suppressed and turned into bouts of depression. From then on, I would go four to five months feeling relatively fine; then, with no warning, I would wake up the next day and feel abysmally depressed. I had no energy, didn't want to get out of bed, and saw no purpose in any of my activities.

To make matters worse, during this time I was pursuing a master's degree in English literature. Many of my studies were in 19th and 20th century literature, much of which is nihilistic and depressing. I had an entire seminar on the works of Matthew Arnold whose melancholic poetry fit exactly into my thinking at the time. I remember reading *The Wasteland* by T. S. Eliot and feeling deeply the futility of life and all human endeavors. A quote I read then from Henry David Thoreau, "The mass of men lead lives of quiet desperation" summed up my feelings exactly.

During the eighteen years this lasted, I was only on a little Tofranil toward the end of the marriage. I consulted a couple of psychiatrists. One told me that my big problem was that I was wasn't getting rid of my anger. He advised me to take up cussing. The other one saw me once a week for one hour; I talked about my pain, but I found little relief.

Toward the end of the marriage, the pain of the depression had escalated to the point that I became suicidal. Once, I checked myself into a state-run mental hospital for four days. Twice, I took an overdose of sleeping pills. There was talk at this time that Lithium and other drugs could have a powerful effect on depression, but my husband strongly advised me against this approach. He thought I should be able to get better without drugs.

Meanwhile, the problems with my husband's temper had not improved. The years of resentment had hardened into a resolve on my part to leave the marriage. I felt that God disapproved of divorce, but at that point I felt it was either divorce or suicide. I boarded a plane for Texas to visit my widowed mother. My husband, who was furious at my leaving against his wishes, filed for divorce on the grounds of desertion. Our children were eighteen and nineteen at this time, so I felt they could take care of themselves.

The depression lifted when I came to stay with my mother in Texas. I thought my problem had been solved. My husband was causing my depressions—get rid of him and I get rid of the depressions. Unfortunately, it was not that simple. I did go quite a while without a spell of depression.

However, when a lawyer to whom I was engaged unceremoniously "dumped" me for no reason that I could discern, I was plunged into another very serious depression. Here, I had left my marriage because I thought my husband was the sole cause of my depression, only to find that the depression was inside me as strong as ever.

For me, this was the last straw—the lowest point. My husband had filed for divorce on grounds of desertion, and the man I thought would take his place decided he'd rather go with someone else. I determined that if I had to endure these periodic depressions for the rest of my life—life was not worth living. I made a conscious, concerted effort to commit suicide.

The two previous attempts at suicide had not been premeditated. This time I went to the library and found out exactly how much Phenobarbital it would take to kill a person. I consulted a rather unsavory physician and lied to him about severe insomnia and my need for Phenobarbital. I planned to take the Phenobarbital at bedtime in order that I would be dead in the morning. My mother was a sound sleeper; to my knowledge, she never checked on me in the middle of the night.

This I very carefully carried out. All I can figure is that God intervened in this situation because my mother *did* check on me in the middle of the night. When she could not wake me up, she called an ambulance that took me immediately to the hospital and pumped my stomach. Today, I am filled with gratitude for this turn of events.

That was my lowest point. I have never again attempted suicide or seriously considered suicide probably because I began taking antidepressant medication immediately and found that it took away the pain. The doctor put me on Lithium, and I was able to function at a normal level again.

Since that time (1976), I have never missed a day of work due to depression. The bouts of depression would come about every four to six months and last usually about three months. While the depression lasted, I would take Lithium and sometimes an antidepressant (Tofranil or Wellbutrin). When I could feel the depression lifting, I would go off the medication. That was my pattern from then on.

The medications had certain side effects that were troubling—severe constipation, hand tremors, and fuzzy thinking, but I felt anything was preferable to the feeling of depression.

During these last nine years, my problems with depression have lessened greatly. In these years I have been regularly attending Alcoholics Anonymous meetings to support the man I loved who happened to be a recovering alcoholic. We married in 1997, and I continued going to A.A. meetings with him. In addition, I began going to Al-Anon meetings.

While I was going to so many Twelve-Step groups, my depression seemed to take a back seat. I would still go back on medication occasionally, but I noted that the depression was definitely better—no suffering.

One day I made the connection that the Twelve Steps were powerful antidotes to depression. I had been making an effort to consciously practice the Twelve-Step principles in all my affairs, and at present I've gone without the need for antidepressant medication longer than ever before. For my depression, the two most healing things I heard in the Twelve-Step meetings were the importance of daily gratitude to God and the necessity of getting rid of resentments.

I decided that a Twelve-Step program exclusively devoted to depression might similarly help others. In A.A. and Al-Anon meetings, I've encountered numerous people (about one in six) who mention that they are also in treatment for depression. I personally know many people who are unable to take conventional antidepressants because of other medical conditions and people who are on prescription antidepressants and still feel very depressed. These people desperately need a program like Depression Anonymous, although anyone suffering from depression could benefit.

— Notes on Appendixes —

The two appendixes, A and B, that follow are included because (1) members should be personally familiar with these principles to monitor their own thinking (2) Depression Anonymous discussion leaders will find excellent subjects for the group at large to investigate and consider.

Appendix C lays out a sample format for Depression Anonymous meetings, along with the Slogans of D.A. and the Rewards of D.A.

APPENDIX A
COGNITIVE BEHAVIOR THERAPY

Cognitive-behavioral therapy (CBT) is a system developed by Aaron Beck of the University of Pennsylvania and is now in use throughout the United States and Europe.[1]

Cognitive behavior therapy (CBT) is based on the foundation that "you are what you think." Or rather, how you feel is a result of how you think about yourself and your life circumstances. This type of therapy proposes that pessimistic thoughts and negative views of life events contribute to depression. According to this theory, people experiencing depression often have:

- A negative view of themselves, seeing themselves as worthless, inadequate, helpless, unlovable and deficient
- A negative view of their environment, seeing it as overwhelming, unsupportive and filled with obstacles
- A negative view of the future, seeing it as hopeless[2]

THE TEN THINKING ERRORS (COGNITIVE DISTORTIONS) IDENTIFIED BY CBT[3]

1. ALL-OR-NOTHING THINKING: You see things only in extremes, black or white. If something isn't done perfectly, it's a total failure.
2. OVERGENERALIZATION: You see a single negative event as the beginning of an unending cycle.
3. MENTAL FILTER: You magnify the negative aspects of a situation and filter out all the positive ones. Your vision of reality becomes darkened like a drop of ink that discolors an entire pitcher of water.

4. DISQUALIFYING THE POSITIVE: You reject anything positive that happens, insisting that it doesn't count.
5. MAGNIFICATION OR MINIMIZATION: You exaggerate the importance of some things (such as your goof-ups) or you inappropriately shrink other things until they appear tiny (your own desirable qualities). You automatically anticipate the worst.
6. JUMPING TO CONCLUSIONS: You make a negative interpretation even though there are no definite facts to support the conclusion.
    6.1. Mind reading. You conclude that someone else is reacting negatively to you without checking it out.
    6.2. Fortune-telling. You are convinced that things will turn out badly. (This is also called "catastrophizing.")
7. EMOTIONAL REASONING: You just assume that your negative emotions necessarily reflect the way things really are.
8. SHOULD STATEMENTS: You use these on yourself as motivation, and they produce guilt. Directing these statements toward others makes you feel anger, frustration, and resentment.
9. LABELING AND MISLABELING: This is an extreme form of overgeneralization. Instead of saying, "I made a mistake," you say, "I'm a loser." Mislabeling can be directed at others also: "He's a jerk!"
10. PERSONALIZATION: You see yourself as the cause of some negative event that really wasn't under your control.

Beck has also identified a number of *depressogenic assumptions*—false belief that set us up for depression:
1. In order to be happy, I have to be successful in whatever I undertake.

2. To be happy, I must be accepted by all people at all times.
3. If I make a mistake, it means I am inept.
4. I can't live without you.
5. If somebody disagrees with me, it means he doesn't like me.
6. My value as a person depends on what others think of me.[4]

---

[1] Members of Depression Anonymous are encouraged to find a therapist trained in this approach.

[2] Keith Kramlinger, M.D., ed., *Mayo Clinic on Depression* (Rochester Minnesota: Mayo Clinic Health Information, 2001) pp. 88-89.

[3] All ten errors are adapted from David D. Burns, M.D., *Feeling Good: The New Mood Therapy* (New York: William Morrow and Co., 1980) pp. 40-41.

[4] Richard O'Connor, Ph.D., *Undoing Depression: What Therapy Doesn't Teach You and Medication Can't Give You* (New York: Little, Brown, and Co., Berkley Books ed., 1999) p. 146.

Appendix B
Learned Optimism

Learned Optimism is the title of a groundbreaking book by Martin Seligman. In his research, he discovered many things of benefit to depressives. Perhaps the most significant is his discovery of what he calls explanatory style:

> Your habitual way of explaining bad events, your explanatory style, is more than just the words you mouth when you fail. It is a habit of thought, learned in childhood and adolescence. Your explanatory style stems directly from your view of your place in the world—whether you think you are valuable and deserving, or worthless and hopeless. It is the hallmark of whether you are an optimist or a pessimist.[1]

Seligman explains that the people who tend to get depressed habitually say to themselves when they encounter misfortune: "It's me, it's going to last forever, it's going to undermine everything I do." Others, who resist giving in to misfortune say: "It was just circumstances, it's going away quickly anyway, and, besides, there's much more in life."[2]

There are three important dimensions to a person's explanatory style: permanence, pervasiveness, and personalization.

PERMANENCE

Pessimists believe the causes of the bad events that happen to them are permanent: The bad events will persist, will always be there to affect their lives. Optimists believe the causes of bad events are temporary. For example, the pessimist would say, "Diets never work," while the optimist would say, "Diets don't work when you eat out."

If you think about bad things in words like *always* and *never*, you have a permanent, pessimistic style. If you think in words like *sometimes* and *lately*, you have an optimistic style.

PERVASIVENESS: SPECIFIC VS. UNIVERSAL

Permanence deals with time. Pervasiveness deals with space. "Universal explanations produce helplessness across many situations and specific explanations produce helplessness only in the troubled area."[3]

Optimists see their troubles as specific to the situation; pessimists generalize their misfortune to see it as occurring everywhere. For example, the optimist who had a bad math teacher might say, "Mr. Jones is unfair," while the pessimist would say, "All math teachers are unfair."[4]

Seligman goes on to say that these two dimensions, permanence and pervasiveness, determine whether or not you have hope. "Finding temporary and specific causes for misfortune is the art of hope."[5] It is essential that depressives do everything they can to increase hope in their lives.

PERSONALIZATION: INTERNAL VS. EXTERNAL

When bad things happen, the pessimist tends to blame himself (internalize) while the optimist tends to blame other people or circumstances (externalize). People who blame themselves when they fail have low self-esteem as a consequence. They think they are worthless, talentless, and unlovable. People who blame external events do not usually lose self-esteem when bad events strike. More insight into personalization is revealed:

Of the three dimensions of explanatory style, personalization is the easiest to understand. After all, one of the first things a child learns to say is "He did it, not me!" Personalization is also the easiest dimension to overrate. It controls only how you *feel* about yourself, but pervasiveness and permanence—the more important dimensions—control what you *do*: how long you are helpless and across how many situations.[6]

Usually it is urged in Depression Anonymous that members take responsibility for their part in a bad situation and not blame others or circumstances. However, depressed people can often take on too much responsibility for painful situations. A balanced view of the situation is called for here.

EXPLANATORY STYLE IS REVERSED FOR GOOD EVENTS

Thus far, explanatory style has only been discussed in relation to bad events. Note that when good things happen, the explanatory styles of optimist and pessimist reverse. The optimist sees a good situation as enduring, pervasive, and brought on by his own skill; the pessimist sees a positive situation as temporary, specific, and caused by external events.

[1] Martin E.P. Seligman, Ph.D., *Learned Optimism* (New York: Alfred A. Knopf, 1991) p. 44.
[2] Seligman, pp. 43-44.
[3] Seligman, p. 47.
[4] Douglas Bloch, M.A., *Healing from Depression: 12 Weeks to a Better Mood* (Berkeley, CA: Celestial Arts, 2002) p. 225.
[5] Seligman, p. 48.
[6] Seligman, p. 50.

APPENDIX C
SAMPLE FORMAT FOR D.A. MEETINGS

Many people would like to start a D.A. group, but they do not know where to begin or what to say in the course of the one-hour meeting.

Following is the procedure that has been used at the Depression Anonymous meeting in Houston, Texas:

Before the meeting, the chairman asks three people in the group to participate—one to read the "Twelve Steps" (page 7), one to read the "Slogans" (page 137) or "Rewards" (page 138),[1] and one to be the leader for the night. (Sometimes the chairman is also the leader.) Then the chairman reads aloud the opening statements.

OPENING STATEMENTS

We welcome you to Depression Anonymous and believe you will find in this fellowship the hope and joy that we have come to experience.

We who live with active depression or the tendency to depression understand your feelings as perhaps few others can. We, too, have known the depths of despair, but in Depression Anonymous, we discovered that it is possible to find peace and happiness in our lives.

This program is not intended to provide medical advice or take the place of medical advice and treatment from personal physicians. Members are advised to consult their own doctors or other qualified health professionals regarding the treatment of their medical problems.

We urge you to try our program; it has helped many of us to recover. Depression Anonymous is based on the Twelve Steps adapted from Alcoholics Anonymous— applied to the special problems we face as depression-prone individuals. The interchange of our experience, hope and love at meetings fortify us against the life-destroying effects of depression.

Like A.A., Depression Anonymous is an anonymous fellowship.

Everything that is said here, in the group meeting and member-to-member, must be held in confidence. However, anyone in a meeting judged to be on the brink of suicide should know in advance that anonymity does not apply in this situation.[2]

We fully expect that those who commit to attending meetings regularly and working the steps will see significant relief from depression. Some will be able to reduce medication.

In our meetings, we do not dwell on the pain of our depression; we focus on the things we have done that brought relief.

The chairman then asks the person designated before the meeting to read the "Twelve Steps".

The chairman asks for the reading of the "Slogans" or the "Rewards".

The chairman says, "We'll now have a moment of silence, followed by
'The Serenity Prayer.'"

> God, grant me the serenity
> To accept the things I cannot change
> Courage to change the things I can,
> And wisdom to know the difference. Amen.

The chairman introduces the meeting's leader who will state the topic for discussion or study.

The leader either introduces a topic for group discussion or directs the study of a particular step (PART ONE) or a personal story (PART TWO) from the D.A. book. One way that the Houston group studies is for each person to have a copy of the chapter. A volunteer starts reading aloud and stops when the text touches on something that he wants to share with the group. Sometimes he will read a sentence, sometimes a paragraph—it does not matter. The important point is to stop and share when something on the page relates to the reader's own experience. (Of course, people in the group can always say, "Pass," if they don't feel like reading or sharing.)

The objective is for the members of the group to share their experience, strength and hope. The personal stories for study introduce new ideas and solutions into the group, ideas that have been tested in the lives of the people reported in PART TWO. Often, the group members will find practical answers to their own problems in studying the life stories of others.

Three or four minutes before the hour is up, the chairman will read aloud the closing statements:

CLOSING STATEMENTS

In closing, I would like to say that the opinions expressed here were strictly those of the people who gave them. Take what is helpful to you and leave the rest.

Begin today to take an active part in your recovery from depression. This means working the steps with a sponsor[3] and a commitment to attend meetings regularly. The suggestion is that you attend at least six meetings in six weeks before you decide whether this program is for you.

The things you heard were spoken in confidence and should be treated as confidential. Talk to each other, but let there be no gossip or criticism of one another. Instead, let the understanding, love and peace of the program shape your outlook on yourself and other people.

The support of the group and the power of God *will* enable you to triumph in your struggle with depression. Remember Step Three—the cornerstone of the program—that our will and our lives are now under the control of God. You are no longer alone in your battle with depression.

Will all who care to join with me in the closing prayer:

Our Father who art in heaven,
Hallowed by thy name.
Thy kingdom come.
Thy will be done
In earth, as it is in heaven.
Give us this day our daily bread.
And forgive us our trespasses, as we forgive
those that trespass against us.
And lead us not into temptation,
But deliver us from evil.
For thine is the kingdom, and the power, and the
glory, for ever. Amen."

---

[1] The Houston group alternates between the Slogans and the Rewards—one week the Slogans will be read, and the next week the Rewards will be read.

[2] We are all bound by law and conscience to report any person to his family or physician who appears to be a danger to himself.

[3] Twelve-step groups urge all newcomers to choose someone in the group they admire to be their sponsor. The newcomer usually simply asks the member he/she has chosen, "Will you be my sponsor?" The sponsor's responsibility is to guide the newcomer through the steps and to be a special friend and advisor.

THE SLOGANS OF
DEPRESSION ANONYMOUS

Let go and let God
Easy does it
First things first
One day at a time
Keep it simple
Have an attitude of gratitude
Don't believe everything you think
Fake it until you make it

DO:

Do forgive—yourself and others.

Do be honest with yourself.

Do take it easy; tension is harmful.

Do play—find recreation and hobbies.

Do learn the facts about the disease of depression.

Do pray.

Do maintain a healthy diet and lifestyle.

Do exercise or take a walk each day.

Do challenge all your negative thinking.

Do engage in activities that were formerly pleasurable.

DON'T:

Don't lose your temper.

Don't wallow in self-pity.

Don't be a doormat.

Don't be discouraged by the mistakes you make.

Don't get stuck in obsessive thoughts.

Don't isolate yourself—you need to be around other people.

Don't be depressed because you're depressed.

THE REWARDS OF
DEPRESSION ANONYMOUS

We have definite rewards from working the Twelve Steps. "If we are painstaking about this phase of our development, we will be amazed before we are half way through.

- We are going to know a new freedom and a new happiness.
- We will not regret the past nor wish to shut the door on it.
- We will comprehend the word serenity.
- We will know peace.
- No matter how far down the scale we have gone, we will see how our experience can benefit others.
- That feeling of uselessness and self-pity will disappear.
- We will lose interest in selfish things and gain interest in our fellows.
- Self-seeking will slip away.
- Our whole attitude and outlook upon life will change.
- Fear of people and of economic insecurity will leave us.
- We will intuitively know how to handle situations which used to baffle us.
- We will suddenly realize that God is doing for us what we could not do for ourselves.

Are these extravagant promises? We think not. . . . **They will always materialize if we work for them."**[*]

---

[*] *Alcoholics Anonymous* (New York: Alcoholics Anonymous World Services, Inc., 2001) pp. 83-84.

— ABOUT THE COVER ARTIST —

LangMarc Publishing is honored to have the permission of award-winning artist Jonathan Qualben of Missoula, Montana, to portray his brilliant sculpture named "Reach" on the cover of *Reach to Recovery: Depression Anonymous*.

Qualben has devised a unique process that allows him to construct elegant wall-hung sculptures using thin layers of concrete. He has captured the expressiveness, grace, and tenuous strength of the animate human form.

He points out that "Sculpture is the art of bringing a moment alive and into focus. It is an idea, a transitory experience, suspended and given permanence."

Qualben's work can be seen in select galleries in the United States and is collected internationally. His sculpture "Affirmation" was accepted as a permanent piece of art at the Carter Center in Atlanta, Georgia. Jonathan traveled to the Center to meet the Carters and view the piece, which is on display in the Office of the Director of Conflict Resolution. Of "Affirmation" Qualben says, "A joyful expression can provide the healing and strength we need in our struggle for peace within ourselves and for our world."

A native of Brooklyn, New York, he relocated to Missoula, Montana in 1983. Since 1994 he has devoted himself to exploring concrete as an artistic medium and developing his own unique application methods and techniques. In 1998, he received the prestigious Montana Individual Artist Fellowship.

Qualben's web site is www.jonathanqualben.com.

— TO ORDER —

REACH TO RECOVERY: DEPRESSION ANONYMOUS
By Marilyn Patterson

If unavailable at your favorite bookstore,
LangMarc Publishing will fill
your order within 24 hours.

— POSTAL ORDERS —

Langmarc Publishing
P.O. Box 90488
Austin, Texas 78709-0488
or call 1-800-864-1648
email: langmarc@booksails.com

Reach to Recovery: USA $13.95 + $2.05 postage
Canada: $17.95 + Postage

Send _____ copies of *Reach to Recovery* to

_____

_____

_____

Phone: _____

Check enclosed: $ _____

Credit Card: # _____

Expires: _____   4-digit # _____